D0629735

The Controversy over the Distribution of Abolition Literature 1830-1860

◆

BY

W. Sherman Savage
Professor of History, Lincoln University
Jefferson City, Missouri

THE ASSOCIATION FOR THE STUDY OF
NEGRO LIFE AND HISTORY, INC.

1938

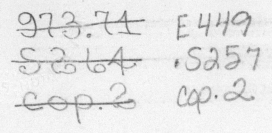

TO MY WIFE
ROENA MUCKELROY SAVAGE

ACKNOWLEDGMENT

My interest in this phase of history began several years ago when pursuing a course in history at the University of Kansas under the direction of the late Professor Frank H. Hodder, who was then head of the Department of History of that institution. In bringing the study to its conclusion I wish to acknowledge aid which has been received from many sources. There are some persons who must be especially mentioned: Professor Hodder, who read the entire manuscript and made several helpful suggestions; Dr. Elmer Ellis of the University of Missouri, Dr. H. H. Simms and Professor Homer C. Hockett of Ohio State University, all of whom have gone over the manuscript at least once; Dr. R. C. Clark of the University of Oregon, who read the first two chapters; and two of my colleagues at Lincoln University, Assistant Professor of History L. J. Greene, who read the manuscript in its early stages, and Assistant Professor of English Armistead Pride, who read the galley proof.

The writer is under a deep sense of gratitude to Dr. Carter G. Woodson, the editor of the series of which this is one volume. He has read the entire manuscript, the galley and page proofs. He has saved the writer many weary hours in seeing this effort through the press.

The publication of this dissertation was made possible by the cooperation of the Association for the Study of Negro Life and History with certain scholars contributing for this purpose twenty-five dollars each and two fraternal organizations appropriating one hundred dollars each. The persons thus assisting were Dr. Lorenzo D. Turner, Dr. Horace M. Bond, Dean A. A. Taylor, President H. Councill Trenholm, and the author himself. The organizations thus cooperating were the Alpha Phi Alpha Fraternity and the Delta Sigma Theta Sorority.

W. Sherman Savage

Jefferson City, Missouri
December, 1938

TABLE OF CONTENTS

INTRODUCTION

The controversy over the use of the Abolition Literature origi-
nated about 1816 and lasted until 1860. It reached its flood tide in
the middle thirties. It has been customary to fix the beginning of
this dispute in 1835—the time of the Charleston *dissension,* which
ended in 1836 with the refusal of Congress to pass any law to
regulate the distribution of literature through the Federal mail.
This was a part of the political and economic history of the period
and was not an isolated event as has been generally supposed.

The purpose of this study is to trace this controversy from
its origin to its conclusion; to ascertain what influence it had upon
the political and economic structure of the country; to show the
motives which actuated the movement; and to give the reason why
the movement broke out in 1835.

The slavery controversy is a vital part of our history from
1820 to 1860. The use of the mail was only one phase of the
slavery affair which agitated this country. Its importance has
been under-estimated because it has been over-shadowed by other
antislavery movements such as the antislavery petitions, coastwise
slave trade, the fugitive slave law, and other aspects which are
better known. The use of the mail was resorted to by the abolition societies in order to reach their objectives and to convert
those persons who were most interested in slavery; namely, the
slaveholders. The means by which they hoped to bring this about
was the establishment of papers which were to be sent through
the Federal mail.

The effort on the part of the abolition societies was in operation before the spring of 1835. There had been established already
papers which had the abolition of slavery as their purpose. The
method used by these papers was to be gradual emancipation
instead of immediate emancipation as was advocated by those
papers which followed later. The first abolition paper was influenced by the Tennessee Manumission Society which was organized at Loose Creek Meeting House, Jefferson County, February 25, 1816, by Charles Osborn, John Canady, John Swain,
Elihu Swain, John Underhill, Jessie Wills, David Maulsby, and

Thomas Morgan.[1] The moving spirit in this organization was
Charles Osborn, who became the first editor of the paper of these
reformers. He soon moved from East Tennessee to Mount
Pleasant, Ohio, where he began the publication of *The Philanthropist*.[2] The purpose of the paper, as set forth in his prospectus, was to discuss slavery and other timely subjects, such as
war and intemperance.[3] The paper revealed that there was little
in it which would offend anyone. The articles on slavery were
for the most part those which were taken from other papers.[4]
The first paper was established in February, 1816, and was dis-
continued in October of the same year. Osborn moved to Indiana, where he spent the rest of his life.[5]

Another moving spirit in this early abolition publication
business was Elihu Embree of Jonesboro, Tennessee. He was
born in Pennsylvania but early moved to Tennessee.[6] He was a
Quaker and early inherited the love of freedom for which that
sect was noted. He took an active part in the manumission society of that state and began the publication of a paper called
Manumission Intelligencer in March 1819, in Jonesboro. It first
came out as a weekly, appearing for about fifty issues.[7] In 1820,
the publication changed its name to *The Emancipator*. The first
number of *The Emancipator* appeared April 30.[8] Under this name
it continued only eight months, for Embree died in 1820. Embree
was an outspoken abolitionist, in Tennessee, ten years before violent
abolition had developed in New England. He felt that slavery was
such a moral evil that it should be abolished. He had as his creed
universal liberty, which he hoped to maintain by offending as few

[1] Rev. E. E. Hoss, *Elihu Embree, Abolitionist*, II.

[2] Benjamin Lundy, *The Life and Travels and Opinions of Benjamin
Lundy*, 18. The paper under the same name lasted down to the Civil War.
It was edited later by Birney and Bailey.

[3] A. E. Martin, ''Pioneer Anti-Slavery Press,'' *Mississippi Valley Historical Review*, II, 511.

[4] The paper had regular columns such as ''Slaveholder's News,'' relating
to abolition, foreign news, etc. This is shown in the first numbers of *The
Philanthropist*.

[5] Rev. E. E. Hoss, *op. cit.*, 11. *Ibid.*, p. 7. He was a Quaker and early
inherited the love of freedom for which they were noted.

[6] C. P. Patterson, *The Negro in Tennessee*, 185.

[7] *Ibid.* There are about 8 or 10 copies of this first paper in the posses-
sion of various individuals of Washington County, Tennessee, Patterson
tells us.

[8] *The Emancipator*, Volume I, No. 1, Jonesboro. There was also *The
New York Emancipator*, published under the editorship of R. G. Williams.

persons as possible.[9] This view he expressed in his second number
of *The Emancipator*, in answer to criticism which had been made of
his paper. Some had thought that he was too mild in his attack
on slavery, while others thought he was too violent. He devoted
the first page of his second number to an expression of his own
point of view in an effort to make his own position clear.

The greater part of this publication discussed the activities
of the Tennessee Manumission Society. The constitution of the
Society was published in the very first number.[10] The paper
touched upon many phases of the slavery question in its various
articles. Like most of the papers of that day, much of the space
was filled with matter from other publications. The fact that the
paper was not as violent as those which followed no doubt accounts
for the little opposition to it at the beginning.

There was another abolitionist, Benjamin Lundy, who con-
tributed much to the early period. His paper was outspoken on
slavery and attracted attention far and wide. Lundy was born
of Quaker parents in New Jersey.[11] In his early as well as his
later life he moved from place to place. It was after he had
married and finally settled at St. Clairsville, Ohio, that he came
in contact with Charles Osborn, who at that time was at Mt.
Pleasant, Ohio, where Lundy wrote several articles for *The Philanthropist*. These articles impressed Osborn so much that he asked
Lundy to collaborate with him in the editorial work of his paper.[12]
Lundy doubted his ability to do the work, but because
of his interest in the question of slavery decided to take it up.
Before he could join in the work, Osborn sold the paper and
moved away, and Lundy gave up the project. About this same
time Embree died, and Lundy decided definitely to go into the
business of publishing an anti-slavery paper. He moved to Mt.
Pleasant and began the publication of the *Genius of Universal
Emancipation*. The first number of the paper appeared in January, 1821. In the prospectus of his paper Lundy said it was
time to speak out against slavery and draw the attention of the

[9] *The Emancipator*, Volume I, No. 2, p. 17, March 31, 1820. It was a
monthly publication, dated the last day of the month.
[10] *The Emancipator*, Volume I, No. 1, p. 11, April 30, 1820. The complete constitution is found in Vol. I, No. 2, May 31, 1820. *The Emancipator*
has been made available in a recent reprint published in Nashville, Tennessee,
by B. N. Murphy.
[11] B. Lundy, *Life of Benjamin Lundy*, 13.
[12] B. Lundy, *Life of Benjamin Lundy*, 13.

people to it.[13] Lundy's paper was so outspoken on slavery that it attracted attention far and wide. He was invited to East Tennessee to take up the work which had been left by Embree. He later moved from East Tennessee to Baltimore, thence to Washington. He traveled widely, mostly on foot, in the interest of his paper, which he printed wherever he was located.

While outspoken, this paper was not violent. It carried the news of slavery in foreign countries; it contained foreign news, personal articles and discussions of questions of the day.[14] Although Lundy was positive in his own mind concerning the evils of slavery, he did not think it could be abolished immediately. Through his work he advocated gradual emancipation.[15] Lundy's paper had a large influence, and he had no difficulty in its distribution.

John Rankin was another in this period who was especially noted in the antislavery cause. He was born in East Tennessee in 1793.[16] After many hardships he entered Washington College in that section, where he prepared for his work. In 1817 he moved to Ohio because of his opposition to slavery.[17] It was about this time that the country was much agitated over the question. The result was the Missouri Compromise. In 1822 Rankin took the pastorate of the Presbyterian Church at Ripley, Ohio. He undertook to prove that slavery was wrong from the point of view of the Bible. He wrote a number of letters to this effect to his brother, Thomas Rankin, in Virginia.[18] He did not confine his activities to the writing of letters, however, but lectured extensively on slavery, in various parts of the country. He also wrote many pamphlets on the subject of slavery, and rested his cause upon the Bible, which he thought showed that man was not made to serve other men.[19] Rankin worked incessantly for the advancement of his ideas. He was the only one of the early abolitionists who lived long enough to see slavery overthrown.

These men have been called mild abolitionists by some because they were not as violent as those who later said that slavery

[13] A. E. Martin, ''Pioneer Anti-Slavery Press,'' *Mississippi Valley Historical Review*, 11, 522.

[14] *Genius of Universal Emancipation*, September, 1829. This is probably not complete in any library.

[15] A. E. Martin, *loc. cit.*, 11, 255.

[16] *Genius of Universal Emancipation*, September, 1829.

[17] *Ibid.*, 17.

[18] John Rankin, *Address to the Churches*, Oberlin Collection, No. 22, p. 56.

[19] *Ibid.*, 56.

must be abolished at any cost. The former group believed that the education of the general public would rid the country of the curse of slavery. The new group also believed in the education of the public. However, it did not want the papers to reach the public by the slow process of chance subscriptions, but saw to it that the public had these papers at its disposal. The papers were sent free to those who did not subscribe. This latter effort laid the basis for the controversy over the use of the mail.

The second period of abolition papers is marked by the publishing of Walker's *Appeal* and *The Liberator*. Walker's *Appeal* made its appearance at Boston in 1829.[20] The editor was David Walker, a free Negro, born in North Carolina in 1785.[21] He was intelligent and had a moderate education.[22] He developed a hatred for slavery as a result of what he saw of it both in his surroundings and in his extensive travels, which had carried him through the South and much of the West. He was very outspoken; he called attention to the Declaration of Independence. He said that the suffering of Americans under Great Britain was not one-tenth as cruel as the suffering of the slaves.[23] He addressed the slaveholder directly and said, "Some of you believe we will not throw off your murderous yoke." Walker informed the slaveowners that he believed they were destined to be sadly fooled.[24] He went still further in this pamphlet and maintained that if the whites wanted slaves and wished to make slaves out of Negroes they would be sorry for it. He was sure they would get enough of making slaves, of butchering and murdering Negroes.[25] These open expressions were addressed to the slaveholder. He expressed his opinion of the slave and the free Negro. He said, "We and our children are brutes and of course are and ought to be slaves to the American people and their children forever, to dig their mines, and work their farms, and then go on enriching them from one generation to another with our blood and our tears."[26] These were bold statements,

---

[20] David Walker, *Appeal*, Part I, p. 1.
[21] W. J. F. Meredith, *The Negro in the Anti-Slavery Movement*. Walker was free because his mother was a free woman; his father was a slave.
[22] S. May, *Recollections*, 133.
[23] Walker, *Appeal*, 78.
[24] *Ibid.*, 79. He said this was true because man could not measure arms with God.
[25] *Ibid.*, 23. He was as sure this would be true as he was that the world existed.
[26] Walker, *Appeal*, 3.

and the South could look at them in no other sense than that they urged the slaves to revolt. There was no doubt that Walker wanted the Negroes to revolt against their masters. This alarmed the South as nothing before had alarmed it. The Governor of Georgia wrote to Harrison G. Otis, Mayor of Boston, requesting him to suppress the *Appeal*. This, of course, the Mayor could not do, for he believed anyone had a right to express his thoughts.[27] A group of men in Georgia offered $10,000 for Walker if he were captured alive and $1,000 if found dead.[28] Walker died soon after, whether by fair or by foul means we do not know. Walker's *Appeal* was outspoken on slavery and had, no doubt, a great influence in moulding the sentiment of the South toward slavery and the antislavery papers which came later.

Another paper which came at this time was *The Liberator* edited by William Lloyd Garrison. The first number of this paper appeared on January 1, 1831, and was printed at Boston.[29] Garrison announced his abolition principles in the first issue of the paper. He said, "Our Country is the world, and our countrymen are all mankind."[30] This motto was carried across the top of each number of *The Liberator*. In an address, which he broadcast over the country, he said he was aware that certain persons would object to the severity of his language, but he had no intention of moderation; on this subject he was as harsh as justice and as uncompromising as truth.[31] This paper, coming as it did after Walker's *Appeal*, was linked with it and was considered in the same class, urging the slaves to revolt. This was denied by Garrison as being far from his purpose, and he condemned the work of David Walker.[32] His idea was the one followed by the antislavery societies; namely, the educating of the public to the evils of slavery.

The Liberator, while it did make harsh statements, had some of the qualifications of a regular paper. It carried letters from individuals, quotations, material on the progress of society, health, and morals, foreign correspondence and the news of the

[27] Meredith, *op. cit.*, 32.

[28] *Ibid.*, 34.

[29] *The Liberator*, Vol. I, No. 1, January 1, 1931. Garrison had been influenced by Lundy, as the two had worked together.

[30] W. P. Garrison, *Life of William Lloyd Garrison*, 1, 219.

[31] *Ibid.*, 225.

[32] S. J. May, *op. cit.*, 133.

antislavery societies.[33] This would seem almost like a present-day paper. Many of these articles from individuals discussed the evils of slavery.[34] Some of the matters which kept recurring were: "Facts showing the safety of emancipation," "The remedy for slavery," and many others of a similar nature. This seems not so unusual but it was considered by both the North and the South as meddling with something which should not concern Garrison. The North did very little about it, but the South offered liberal rewards if Walker and Garrison were apprehended and turned over to authorities in the latter section. Governor Lumkin of Georgia gave his approval to an act of the legislature offering $4,000 to anyone who would arrest and bring to trial under the laws of the state of Georgia the editor of *The Liberator*.[35] The vigilance committee, composed of a body of gentlemen of the highest respectability of the city of Columbia, South Carolina, offered $1,500 for the apprehension and prosecution to conviction of any white person detected in the act of distributing or circulating within the state of South Carolina *The Liberator* printed in Boston by Garrison and Knapp, or Walker's *Appeal,* or any other paper of a similar nature.[36] This was one way the South tried to control those papers which it considered as urging insurrection.

This is the first phase of the controversy over antislavery papers. It lasted throughout the entire period of slavery, much longer than any other single phase of the antislavery movement. The movement began before the Missouri Compromise and did not end until the very end of the Civil War.

[33] *The Liberator*, February 7, 1835. This is a sample of the type of news it carried.
[34] *Ibid.*
[35] W. Goddell, *Slavery and Anti-Slavery*, 410.
[36] H. M. Henry, *Police Control of Slaves in South Carolina*, 156. He takes this item from *Southern Times and State Gazette*, October 8, 1831. The Association announced its program September 28, 1831.

The Controversy over the Distribution of Abolition Literature 1830-1860

CHAPTER I

THE INFLUENCE OF THE EARLY INSURRECTIONS ON THE ATTITUDE TOWARD ANTI-SLAVERY PAPERS

The South was disturbed from 1830 to 1835 not only by the papers but also by insurrections or attempted insurrections, which were attributed to the papers. One of the most important and far-reaching of these and one which influenced the South tremendously, was the Denmark Vesey Insurrection. Vesey was a free Negro who lived in the city of Charleston, South Carolina. In 1822 he planned an uprising not only in Charleston but for forty or fifty miles around the city.[1] He hoped to gain control of the shipping in the harbor, and if hard pressed, to sail to the West Indies where he would be protected by the English or French law.[2] This plot was well worked out, and every one who was enlisted was pledged to secrecy. It would have succeeded but for a house servant.[3] The fact that the plan so nearly succeeded brought home to the South more emphatically the danger in the slaves and in free Negroes if they were tampered with.

This episode had been closed but a short time when another uprising, the Nat Turner Insurrection, more successful than the Vesey uprising, occurred near Southampton, Virginia, on August 21, 1831. Nat Turner was born of Negro slave parents in Virginia about 1800.[4] It is said his mother taught him that he, like Moses, was to lead his people out of slavery.[5] This might

[1] A. B. Hart, *Slavery and Abolition*, 153.
[2] *Negro Year Book*, 1825-26, 214, M. W. Work, editor; Department of Records and Research, Tuskegee Institute. The slaves were constantly revolting. It is estimated there were 25 insurrections before the American Revolution.
[3] *Ibid.*, 213. This case comes before our period but influenced the South to such an extent that it may account for the attitude toward Walker's *Appeal*. Insurrections were much more prevalent than has been supposed. Monroe Work lists 34 of the most important ones.
[4] *Harper's Encyclopedia of United States History*, IX. The age is only approximate, for no record was kept of the birth of slaves.
[5] *Negro Year Book*, 1925-26, 214.

1

have had much to do with his action. Nat Turner was endowed with a natural intelligence and quickness possessed by few men, with a mind capable of high attainment. He read the Bible and every book which came in his way.[6] He fancied that he was called by God and that he heard voices and read messages on the leaves and in the sky directing him to free his people.[7]   This he would do by murdering the slave owners. The motives for Turner's action were both religious and intellectual.

The insurrection broke out on Sunday night, August 21, 1831. This was easily accomplished because at that time many of the whites were away attending a camp meeting.[8] Turner first took the life of his own master and his family and then went from farm-house to farm-house until between fifty and sixty persons, men, women, and children, were killed. The insurrection was put down, and most of the Negro slaves captured in a short time. (Turner, however, was not captured until November the fourth.)[9] It was shown that he had not been at any time more than five miles away from the plantation. These Negro slave leaders were put to death; others were transplanted.[10] This was the most appalling of all the insurrections among the slaves.

The Nat Turner Insurrection was only a part of a plan for a general uprising, some have claimed. There were attempted or supposed insurrections in Maryland and in various parts of North Carolina.[11] The information came to a gentleman in Norfolk in a letter dated October the fourth, 1831, from Cambridge, Maryland, relating the arrest of a white woman for tampering with the slaves and inciting them to insurrection.[12] This woman was arrested in North West Fork Bridge, 22 miles from Cambridge, and lodged in jail. In North Carolina, a letter to the Norfolk *Herald* denoted the great excitement in Winston, North

[6] W. S. Drewry, *The Southampton Insurrection*, 112.

[7] F. Bancroft, *Slave Trading in the Old South*, 19.

[8] U. B. Phillips, *American Negro Slavery*, 480. Probably more would have been killed if the whites had been home. Phillips says ten men, fourteen women and thirty-one children were killed.

[9] *Richmond Enquirer*, November 8, 1831.

[10] Bancroft, *op. cit.*, 481.

[11] Drewry, *op. cit.*, 155. Princess Anne, Somerset County, Maryland, and the black belt of North Carolina.

[12] *Ibid.*, 150. She was reported by a Negro slave. It was claimed that she told the Negroes if they wanted arms to write to the Bishop of the Bethelemite church in Philadelphia. This was overheard by slave masters in the house where the woman met the Negroes.

Carolina, because of the fear of insurrection among the slaves.[13] The rumor spread to Milledgeville, Georgia, the capital of the state on October 4, 1831, that the Negroes were rising, but this rumor proved false.[14] Much preparation was made for the protection of the capital city and the subjection of the Negroes, who never came. It was further rumored in Baltimore, that Raleigh and Wilmington, North Carolina, were in the hands of Negro slaves and were burned.[15] In spite of these various attempts or supposed attempts on the part of Negroes to revolt there seems to be no evidence of concerted action in relation to the Nat Turner Insurrection.[16] It is almost certain that Nat Turner talked it over with his friends and those who were to have a part in the plot. Turner believed he was inspired, that it was God's will, and he probably depended little upon man.

Another motive which has been given for this uprising was the abolition papers. Some of the papers were violent and urged the slaves to revolt. Did these papers reach Nat Turner; and if so, did they influence his actions on August 21? Drewry said that a white man, Bradley, was known to have been very intimate with Turner.[17] This incident and the fact that he read everything which came his way are taken as proof that he received and read these papers and that they influenced the insurrection. These papers were circulated through the mail as early as 1831. The mail was not the only means used to reach the slaves. Ministers of the gospel secretly communicated with the slaves and sent back to the North accounts of their treatment.[18] Governor Floyd of Virginia in his message to the legislature of his state placed the blame for the insurrection in Southampton on pamphlets of the North reaching the slaves through agents and the post office.[19] He recommended that the Negro preachers be

[13] Drewry, *op. cit.*, 150. This letter was dated August 24, 1831, three days after the insurrection.

[14] Phillips, *op. cit.*, 282.

[15] *Niles Register*, XLI, 55. This letter was to a Mr. Harnum of the City Hotel, Baltimore, dated September 13, 1831. There was a demand, this letter said, for arms from Johnson County near Raleigh because of a supposed uprising among the Negroes.

[16] *Richmond Enquirer*, September 30, 1891, Editorial. The view was given in the testimony of a woman belonging to Mr. Salmon Parker of Southampton. She claimed she had heard the subject discussed several months before.

[17] *Op. cit.*, 140.

[18] *Ibid.*, 149. Another source for this literature was by peddlers and women. This was all done secretly.

[19] *Richmond Enquirer*, December 2, 1831. Walker's *Appeal* had been sent since 1829, but *The Liberator* had been in operation only since 1831.

silenced because they exerted too much influence over their fellows. His reason for this recommendation was the fact that he considered the Negro preacher a distributor of an objectionable type of literature. Governor Roman of Louisiana called the legislature in special session for the purpose of handling the matter of slave insurrection. He thought these insurrections were instigated primarily by propagandists and people setting forth false ideas of philanthropy.[20] There is no exact proof that these papers reached the slaves, in spite of the assertions of those governors. The papers did circulate, but whether they reached Nat Turner or not has not been proved.

If these papers did not reach the slaves, the masters chose to think so and passed much legislation during this early period to curtail real or possible uprisings. The Virginia Legislature in response to its governor's recommendation passed a new law to control slaves. Neither slaves nor free Negroes were allowed to preach. The penalty for the violation of this law was thirty-nine stripes by the justice of the peace or any person who wished to give them.[21] The law also made it illegal for any person to circulate incendiary literature in the state of Virginia. If the offender was a Negro, his punishment for the first offence was whipping, with as many lashes as those in charge felt he deserved.[22] Death was the penalty for the second violation. The punishment for the white person who might be guilty of this crime was a fine of not less than $100 nor more than $1,000. This law was drastic, but its purpose was to make it impossible for another uprising such as the Nat Turner Insurrection.

Louisiana, in response to its governor, passed a law to strengthen its slave code.[23] The act which was passed made it

[20] *Richmond Enquirer*, December 8, 1831; Niles Register, XLI, 350. Message delivered on December 12.
[21] *Acts of Virginia*, 1832, Sec. 1, 20. Approved March 16, 1832. It made it unlawful for slaves to attend meetings at night even if held by a white minister. Section 2.
[22] *Ibid.*, Sec. 7, 21. Another act was passed at this time relating to slaves in Northampton County. That county asked the general assembly for permission to borrow $15,000 to remove the slaves from that county. They were to pay it by taxing themselves. The legislature approved the act. This shows how slavery influenced the society of the state. A petition was procured from citizens of Hanover County signed by several slave owners praying that the legislature should take means to remove all free Negroes and Mulattos and other such people as may come to the state. This was discussed in the legislature but was rejected by a vote of 99-27. *Richmond Enquirer*, December 15, 1831.
[23] *Acts of Louisiana*, 1832, 140.

unlawful for any one to introduce slaves from the border states, for it was feared that slaves from these states would cause the slaves of Louisiana to revolt. The state legislature did not pass as drastic a law as might have been expected from the tone of the governor's message. The legislature depended upon the laws then in force. Kentucky also did not pass any law but depended upon its laws of 1799 to take care of any emergency.[24] North Carolina, where riots occurred or the fear of them was greatest, passed in 1831 a law which made it unlawful under any pretense whatsoever for a slave or a free Negro to preach or exhort in public or to act as a teacher or preacher at a prayer meeting. The state made the offense for this thirty-nine lashes for both the slave and free Negro.[25] The difference in punishment came in that the slave was given thirty-nine lashes for the first offense; the free Negro was given thirty-nine lashes for each offense. The law of 1831 was drastic enough, because it provided that if any slave or free Negro should revolt or be connected with any plot or conspiracy for the purpose of revolting, he would suffer death or transportation from the state.[26] North Carolina, like Virginia, had placed the cause for the revolt in Virginia and for the supposed insurrection in North Carolina at the door of the Negro preacher and thus passed a law to prohibit and suppress this evil.

The state of Georgia was faced with the same problem as the other states; however, it did not pass a general law. Georgia relied upon the method of passing local laws. Such a law was passed for Milledgeville in 1831 which placed the blame for the trouble in that town upon the fact that the slaves were hired out and lived away from their masters.[27] Under this law slaves must not be hired out and must live with their masters. South Carolina, like Georgia, passed no definite law to control incendiary literature, but depended upon the law of 1820, which was very drastic; it stipulated in effect that any white man caught circulating any written or printed paper with the intent

[24] *Digest of Statutes of Kentucky*, 11, 1472. Law of 1798, Sec. 7. Took up the matter of controlling abolitionists.

[25] *Revised Statutes of North Carolina*, 1836-37, p. 580, Sec. 34 of the slave law—passed 1831.

[26] *Revised Statutes of North Carolina*, 1836-37, p. 580, Sec. 35 of the act related to slavery, passed in 1802. The legislature of 1831 also passed an additional law.

[27] *Acts of Georgia*, 1831, 223. Act passed December 27. Acts were passed at the same time to regulate the slaves at Jefferson, Burke and Screven. *Ibid.*, 226.

to disturb the peace and security of slaves was to be punished. The penalty for such offense, regardless of whether the papers were distributed directly or indirectly, was a fine of one thousand dollars and imprisonment for a period not exceeding one year.[28] A free Negro was given for his first offense a fine of $1,000, for his second offense fifty lashes and banishment from the state; should he return he would suffer death.[29] Alabama passed no law in 1831 but did pass one in 1833 that had for its purpose regulating the action of slaves. The law said those who should teach the slaves to write must pay a fine of from $250 to $500. This same law made it unlawful for as many as five Negroes to assemble.[30] With laws already existing this was sufficient for the control of antislavery agitation in Alabama.

The last state to be considered with reference to this matter is Tennessee. Faced with this problem of making some law to control more effectively slaves and free Negroes, the legislature passed a law which made it unlawful for slaves to hold assemblies at unusual times and places.[31] It was the duty of any sheriff or justice of the peace to disperse them, and if they did not disperse within a reasonable time they were to be punished. The act controlling rebellion was emphasized and discretionary power was granted the court trying a case of rebellion as to whether it would inflict death or lashes and the pillory.[32] When the court had rendered a decision in an insurrection case there could be no appeal.[33] The state of Tennessee made its law very drastic in order to bring these insurrections to a close.

The Nat Turner Insurrection had an economic significance. Slavery in Virginia, as in Missouri, was becoming somewhat unprofitable because cotton was not grown to a large extent in the state. The economic importance of this riot was pointed out by Thomas Dew. He said that the Southampton massacre had produced great excitement and apprehension throughout the slaveholding states and that the sale of those slaves from Virginia had been

---

[28] *Statutes at Large of South Carolina*, VII, 460. Law of 1820 relating to slaves, Sec. VI.

[29] *Ibid.*, 370. He was not even to be allowed the benefit of clergy. This law seemed ample to take care of Negro revolts.

[30] *Digest of Laws of Alabama*, Sec. 31, "Law on Slavery," 307.

[31] *Public Acts of Tennessee*, 1831, Chap. CIII, Sec. 1.

[32] *Public Acts of Tennessee*, 1831, Chap. CIII, Sec. 4.

[33] *Ibid.*, Sec. 6. Maryland passed a law that free Negroes must leave the state or pay a penalty. *Laws of Maryland*, 1831-32, Chap. 323, Sec. 8.

prohibited by severe penalties.[34] This excitement made the Virginia slave less valuable than other slaves in the open market.

The insurrection in the states had thus been answered by drastic laws. All of the southern states took cognizance of the matter by passing new laws or strengthening old ones. Those states where insurrections had occurred passed the most drastic laws of all. It is not proved that the abolitionist papers were the cause of the insurrections; but some of the states took measures to stop papers from reaching their slaves, and others passed measures to silence the Negro preacher and to prevent assemblies.

In spite of the laws which were passed by the states, there was still a fear of insurrection among the inhabitants of the southern states. The next serious alarm occurred in 1836 near Vicksburg, Mississippi. Little has been made of this affair because it occurred about the same time that the state was making an effort to get rid of its gamblers.[35] According to a report, a white man named Murrel planned a general uprising of the slaves from Maryland to Louisiana. The first attack was to have been made on July 4, 1835, and was prevented only because the matter was overheard in the conversation of slaves. December 25 was then set for a general uprising.[36] The Negroes were to start in Madison County, Mississippi, and to kill all the whites on their way and march to New Orleans. This plot was revealed by a certain Stuart who was later proved to have made up the story.[37] He had quarreled with Murrel, who was his partner in a counterfeiting ring and devised this method of enriching himself. He was not disappointed for everywhere he was received for a time with a manifestation of public gratitude.[38]

The southern people thought that the story was true and it had much influence on the attitude of the South toward abolition papers. Extracts from a letter sent to Garrison addressed at Canton, Mississippi, July 3, said that the Negroes were about

[34] R. Dew, *Review of Debates in the Virginia Legislature*, 50.

[35] *Niles Register*, XLVIII, 439.

[36] *The Liberator*, August 8, 1835.

[37] *Richmond Enquirer*, August 4, 1835. Murrel was a notorious criminal, a horse thief, who seems to have traveled from Maryland to Louisiana during this period, but it is not proved that he tampered with the slaves.

[38] J. H. Claiborne, *Life and Correspondence of John Quitman*, 138. He called Stuart a notorious scamp.

to rise against the whites. The whole country was alarmed.[39] One man who plotted with Negroes was arrested. A court was called immediately; he was found guilty and was put to death. A Negro in Vicksburg was given six hundred lashes until he confessed that the Negroes were to rise on the Fourth of July. As a result of this excitement about ten whites and twelve Negroes were put to death.[40] The whole affair struck fear in the South, and caused extraordinary methods to be used. It is called by one the most extraordinarily lamentable hallucination of that time.[41] Still another thought that while there had been excesses such methods would have a wholesome effect. It would serve as a warning to the abolitionists not only of their own danger but of the great injury they were doing the Negro by meddling with affairs of the South.[42]

This was noticed in another way. Governor Rummel of Mississippi issued an order to control the affair.[43] The proclamation said it had been represented to the Executive that there was a band of lawless, base, villainous, white men traversing the country endeavoring to get up an insurrection. He called upon all citizens to help put it down. The governor thought that it was a widely spread conspiracy.[44] This shows the extent to which this talk of insurrections was believed.

Laws which were passed during this period from 1820-1835 show how much the South feared insurrection. They also give the attitude of the South on the eve of the new crusade of the abolition societies. There was a constant fear in the South of insurrection. These uprisings showed that in spite of the laws they did occur and were likely to occur at any time. It is not surprising that the South took such precautions and resented anything that seemed to interfere with its institutions.

[39] *Ibid.*, 138. The greatest excitements were in the central counties of Mississippi.
[40] *The Liberator*, August 1, 1835.
[41] *Boston Daily Advertiser and Patriot*, August 7, 1835.
[42] Claiborne, *op. cit.*, 138.
[43] *The Liberator*, August 8, 1835. A copy of the governor's proclamation is given.
[44] Prentis, *Memoirs*, 161. Letter to his mother and sister at Vicksburg, September 10, 1835. He agreed that the treatment was harsh.

CHAPTER II

THE PAPERS AT FLOOD TIDE

In the midst of this confusion and fear over the insurrections, the American Anti-Slavery Society announced a new and more effective program as follows:

1. We shall organize Anti-Slavery Societies, if possible, in every city, town and village in our land.

2. We shall send forth agents to lift up the voice of remonstrance, of warning, of entreaty, and rebuke.

3. We shall circularize unsparingly and extensively Anti-Slavery tracts and periodicals.

4. We shall enlist the pulpit and the press in the cause of the suffering and the dumb.

5. We shall aim at a purification of the churches from all participation in the guilt of slavery.

6. We shall encourage the use of free laborers rather than that of slaves by giving preference to their productions.

7. We shall spare no exertions nor means to bring the whole nation to a speedy repentance.[1]

This program was published in the form of an address and sent far and wide in order that the new program might be known. In the first annual report of the American Anti-Slavery Society the committee on publicity insisted that the press was one of the most powerful agencies of reform and said that the society had made as much use of it as possible. The committee informed the society that because of the condition of the treasury not as much use had been made of the press as had been hoped, yet five numbers of the *American Anti-Slavery Reporter,* a monthly magazine, had been published.[2] Most of these magazines had been sent to the South without charge.

The American Anti-Slavery Society and other antislavery

[1] Garrison's *Garrison,* 1, 219.
[2] American Anti-Slavery Society, *First Annual Report,* 1834, 41. Five thousand copies had been printed at the time of the meeting, three thousand had been given away; the rest were on hand.

societies had established a number of other papers, the most noted being *The Emancipator, Slaves' Friend, Anti-Slavery Record, Human Rights,* in addition to *The Liberator.*[3] The papers were purely for the purpose of arousing sentiment against slavery, but were they as vicious as they have been painted? The papers in their entirety have passed away but here and there a copy can be found. *The Emancipator* for June, 1836, discussed a number of subjects on slavery. "Spirit of Slavery," "Communication from Individuals," "Criticism of the Slave System," are only some of the articles published in this number. The motto which the paper took was "To Proclaim Liberty throughout All the Land unto All the Inhabitants Thereof."[4] It also carried other news of a general nature. *The Emancipator* was about as moderate as the papers of that time were. *The Slaves' Friend* was a little pamphlet about two inches by four. It carried pictures which portrayed the cruelty of masters toward their slaves. On the front page of the first number of the volume for 1836, there was a picture of a slave being whipped by his master. There also were little dialogues easily comprehensible to the slave. An example of this is, "What Color was Adam?"[5] Most of the questions had to do either with the color or the condition of the Negro.

The *Anti-Slavery Record* was another antislavery paper published at this time by the American Anti-Slavery Society. It depended upon pictures much as the *Slaves' Friend,* but was larger and the articles were addressed to the adult mind. The number for April, 1836, carried a picture of a white man drowning and a Negro jumping in to rescue him as an illustration of the kindness of Negroes to their masters in spite of their treatment. Another article in this same number, "Facts Showing the Safety of Emancipation," shows how emancipation had worked in Santo Domingo. It was thought that Congress would pass such a law and emancipate the slaves. This small number took up another subject which was objectionable to the South; the wisdom of amalgamation.[6] These are the kinds of articles which ran through the paper and they explain the attitude to-

---

[3] *The Emancipator,* 1, 95. Edited by R. G. Williams, $2.00 a year.
[4] *Ibid.,* 1, 95.
[5] *Slaves' Friend,* volume for 1836. The pamphlet contained about 12 pages. The price was 10 cents per dozen, 80 cents per hundred, and $8.65 per thousand.
[6] *Anti-Slavery Record,* 11, No. 1.

ward it. The paper in most of its numbers insisted that Congress had the authority to abolish slavery in the District of Columbia. The fourth of these papers authorized at this time was *Human Rights*, a monthly tract of four pages. The subjects which it treated were very simple ones, such as liberty of the press and freedom of speech. "How Mobs Are Got Up" was the title of one article which appeared in the February number, 1836.[7] The subject was treated in a very simple manner.

Aside from the subject of slavery, these papers discussed the topics of the day just as any other papers did; and nowhere did they appear to advise the slaves to revolt. Those that were available to the writer did not show the tendency complained of by the South. The pictures were more dangerous in effect than the news, for most of the slaves could not read. While the papers were objectionable to the South, there is little to account for the confusion over them. The reason must be found in the uprisings and the attitude of the South toward them, and the attitude toward Walker's pamphlet which did advise the slaves to revolt.

There was always fear of insurrection. A letter to J. H. Hammond from Henry I. Nott, of Columbia, South Carolina, said that the country was flooded with these incendiary papers. The excitement, he thought, was caused by fear after the Southampton affair.[8] Most of the resolutions and condemnations said that the abolition societies were sending these papers into the midst of the slaves for the purpose of causing insurrection.

The serious effort made by the South to control the flow of the papers has been set forth, and we have observed the accusation made against the abolition societies. What was the purpose of this crusade? Did any of these papers reach the slaves? The society set forth its program in its first annual report. It was the duty of every Christian denomination, it said, to do what it could for the immediate abolition of slavery. Samuel May, speaking before this same meeting, outlined his plan for conducting his campaign for the abolition of slavery. The weapon, he said, must not be the cannon but an appeal to the conscience of the

[7] *Human Rights*, 1, No. 8. Some copies of all of these are in the Library of Congress but not complete. Another magazine was the Quarterly *Anti-Slavery Magazine* which had much the same tenor as other publications. The introduction in the first volume dealt with slavery as a wrong. "Slavery Wrong in Great Britain," "Slavery Tested by its Own Standards." The latter was an article written by William Goodell.

[8] *Hammond Papers*, Vol. VI, March 8, 1836, Columbia, S. C.

slaveholders.[9] By the declaration of their own leaders, there was no intention of giving these papers to the slave. In an address of the American Anti-Slavery Society to the public in 1835, it (the American Anti-Slavery Society) complained that it had been accused of sending publications to slaves for the purpose of stirring up insurrection.[10] The society denied both charges and said the papers were not intended for slaves; if they had been the slaves could not read them and would find no encouragement in them which would cause them to revolt. The society went still further to prove that the slaves did not get these publications. The secretary of the American Anti-Slavery Society received a letter from a gentleman who said his daughter had written him stating that Negroes were being sent abolition papers and that the mayor had a paper urging the Negroes to insurrection. The secretary asked that a copy of this paper be sent him, and if this were true he would resign.[11] He did not get the paper and took it for granted that none were reaching the slaves.

The proslavery leaders did not fear the circulation of the papers in their section of the country. Calhoun said that it was not in the slaveholding section that he feared the effect of abolition literature. It could not be circulated there because of the strict regulations which the South had adopted. It was the effect in the North he dreaded, for there the societies were infusing a deadly poison in the minds of the people.[12] This, he thought, tended to breed hatred between the sections and to split sections into factions. Senator Black, of Mississippi, gave expression to practically the same view in the course of a debate on the floor of the Senate. He said the papers were not circulated in the South, for they could not enlighten that section. It would seem that few of these papers reached the slaves, for most of the avenues were closed. It is almost certain that none of them reached the slaves through the medium of the post office, because the postmaster could not deliver them; however, a few of these may have reached the slaves by other methods. Nehemiah Adams said that cuts and pictures appeared on handkerchiefs used by southern children and slaves.[13] The slaves

[9] *Address of the American Anti-Slavery Society to the Public*, 1835, American Anti-Slavery Society, *Second Annual Report*, 8.
[10] *Address of the American Anti-Slavery Society to the Public*, 1835, American Anti-Slavery Society, Second Annual Report, 8.
[11] *Fourth Annual Report*, Massachusetts Anti-Slavery Society, 21, Note.
[12] Hunt, *John C. Calhoun*, 1, 385.
[13] *South Side View of Slavery*, 188: R. M. Ormsby, *The Whig Party*, 272.

were not so stupid, although some of them could not read, but that if the papers came within their reach, the contents were soon known to them. It might be reasonable to conclude that none of these papers reached the slaves by means of the post office, but the post office was not the only carrier.

In the year 1835, when the controversy was at its height, the number of these publications reached a total of over a million.[14] This was the banner year, for the papers never reached such a high level again. The next year these periodicals had decreased from over a million to less than eight hundred thousand.[15] The reason given for this decrease was that more attention had been given to lectures than in the previous year. This was necessary in order to present the case of the abolitionists and convert the North to their program. Another problem, one for the lecturer rather than for the papers, was that of raising funds for the support of the organization and for the formation of new societies. These lecturers took on another responsibility, that of instructing the Negroes who had recently come North how to adjust themselves to their new surroundings.[16] This shows the reason why less attention was paid to the papers than formerly. It must not be supposed that any of these papers ceased publication, but they did decrease from year to year.

The publications were reaching the South in large numbers. We are told by the *Enquirer* on July 31, 1835, that the first number of *Human Rights* had arrived in Richmond.[17] The same

[14] American Anti-Slavery Society, *Third Annual Report*, 1836, 3.

Human Rights, about 20,000 per month	240,000 per year
Anti-Slavery Record, 25,000 per month	385,000 per year
Emancipator, 15,000 per month	210,000 per year
Slave's Friend, 15,000 per month	205,000 per year
Quarterly Anti-Slavery	5,500 per year
Life of Greenville Sharpe, 2,000 per month	2,000 per year
Bound Volumes	1,000 per year
Mrs. Child's Appeal	1,000 per year
Slaves' Friend (bound volume)	5,000 per year
Occasion Pamphlet	8,500 per year
Circulars	36,000 per year

Total _____ 1,095,800 per year

[15] American Anti-Slavery Society, *Fourth Annual Report*, 1837, 32. Total for this year was 718,267.

[16] *Ibid.* This report said that 483 societies had been organized during the year, and 1,006 societies were flourishing.

[17] Editorial of July 31, 1835. This copy was picked up on the steamer *Kentucky* lost by some one on board from Norfolk to Richmond. It was rumored they were scattered.

Enquirer tells of a bundle of these papers received at the post office in Norfolk. The statement was made by the paper that these documents were addressed to free Negroes.[18] The town became excited and called a meeting, but it was soon found that this was a mistake. The *Herald* opposed the discussion of antislavery papers because it feared that such an act would give too much prominence to the abolitionists. Mobile complained that the papers were reaching the post office there, and one of the periodicals of that city suggested that a meeting should be called to handle the matter.[19] In South Carolina near Charleston a man by the name of Brady stopped at a blacksmiths' shop where slaves were working and asked the slaves to take part in an uprising which he contemplated. A slave reported the affair to his master. Brady was arrested and was fortunate to escape with his life.[20] The *Winchester Virginia Republican*, August 27, 1835, complained of an antislavery agent who entered the town of Shepherdstown on the Potomac in the county of Jefferson, distributed a large number of abolition papers, and escaped without being detected.[21] There was much excitement in Jefferson County, which was literally flooded with these objectionable papers. The city of Savannah was the recipient of such missiles also. When the steamboat arrived from New York many of the abolition papers were on board.[22] The suggestion was made that most of the papers should be sent back and thus impress upon the American Anti-Slavery Society the futility of sending the papers to the South. Near Enfield, North Carolina, several of the abolition papers were picked up along the road. They were apparently dropped by someone traveling south in the stage.[23] Several of the post offices of North Carolina also complained about the receipt of the papers. The *Southern Patriot* gives an account of abolition papers in the city of Nashville. These caused excitement similar to that occasioned in other

---

[18] *Richmond Enquirer*, July 31, 1835. This was quoted from the *Norfolk Herald*. The *Enquirer* of August 4, 1835, retracted its statement because the *Herald* admitted it was mistaken and these papers were not sent to free Negroes, but a large portion were addressed to the most respectable citizens in Norfolk. This mistake was made because the names of the free Negroes had been written upon the magazine.

[19] *Mobile Commercial Register*, August 10, 1835.

[20] *Southern Patriot*, August 22, 1835.

[21] *Ibid*, September 3, 1835.

[22] *Savannah Republican*, August 10, 1835.

[23] *Ibid.*, August 3, 1835.

cities and were called inflammatory papers of the most seditious nature. All of this meant that the ''fanatics'' were moving with concerted action against the South.[24] A large box of these papers was found upon the wharf in Philadelphia. These were seized by the citizens, taken out in the middle of the Delaware, and thrown overboard.[25]

The last incident in the distribution of the antislavery papers to be treated occurred in Charleston. This distribution attracts more attention because Charleston took positive and definite action to stop it. The *Southern Patriot* gave the information that the steamer *Columbia* came loaded with the *Anti-Slavery Record*, the *Emancipator*, and the *Slaves' Friend*, and the editor expressed much concern about the matter. He said if the general post office could not act then the local authorities should.[26] Unless something was done it was impossible to protect the mail. These papers were not all for Charleston, or even for South Carolina, but were for sections of the South and West. The *Patriot* made the pertinent suggestion that those sections of the country which had interests the same as those of South Carolina should act in unison with the state.[27] The people of Charleston were very much excited. On the night of July 29, 1835, a meeting was called, and in all probability measures would have been taken to control the circulation of the abolition papers through the post office of that city but the lieutenant of the city guard persuaded the people to disperse.[28] He felt that the excitement was so fearful it would not be advisable to attempt to take up the matter at that time. Some of the group voted to take the law into their own hands immediately. They visited the post office of that city, forced open the shutter, and secured the objectionable papers which were destined for distribution in the South and West.[29] The abolitionist papers were burned on the evening of July 30, publicly, and many of the most influential citizens attended the meeting. This extreme action gave Charleston more attention than the rest of the cities. Alfred Huger,

[24] July 18, 1835. Quoted from *Nashville Banner*.
[25] *Boston Daily Advertiser*, August 29, 1835.
[26] July 29, 1835.
[27] *Niles Register*, XLVIII, 482.
[28] J. B. MacMaster, *History of the People of the United States*, VI, 257.
[29] *Niles Register*, XLVIII, 403. This paper gives the 30th. Some call it the 29th. Huger, letter to Kendall, July 30, 1835. *Richmond Enquirer*, August 25, 1835.

who was postmaster in Charleston, appointed in January, 1835, recognized his obligation to his government and to the community in which he lived.[30] On July 29, when there was much excitement in Charleston, Huger wrote Postmaster-General Amos Kendall and related to his chief the arrival of abolition papers of the most inflammatory nature which had a tendency to stir up insurrection. He further said that the office in Charleston was literally filled with pamphlets and tracts, and that he had given the subject much thought but was sure those to whom the papers were addressed could suffer no harm if they were deprived of the use of them for a few days. Huger realized he was stretching his authority but assumed the responsibility and asked for instructions from Kendall. The reason for his decided action was the safety of the mail.[31] Huger kept the papers until he had received communication from the Postmaster-General.

The next day Huger wrote his chief again to relate to him what had happened. The excitement was greater than the Charleston postmaster had expected it would be. It had seized all parties and every grade of society. Huger had done all he could to protect the mail; he had remained at the post office late in the evening until all seemed quiet. He said it was hard to see how the outrage could have been prevented. The leading men of both political parties had waited upon Huger in reference to the mail, but he assured them that he would assume the responsibility for non-delivery until he could get instructions from the Postmaster-General.[32] The leading citizens had agreed to this proposition, yet had broken into the post office and taken the papers. Another reason why he took the responsibility was that he feared the rest of the mail would be treated as the papers were treated. He closed by reminding Kendall that he was awaiting anxiously his instructions. This public servant was so anxious to do his duty that when he had been informed where the seized mail was (it had not yet been burned), he told his chief he would consult the District Attorney to ascertain if any arrests could be made.[33] He did this when he realized the whole community was against him.

[30] *Mobile Commercial Register*, January 9, 1835.
[31] Letter from Huger to Kendall, July 20, 1835. Complete correspondence in *Richmond Enquirer*, August 25, 1835.
[32] Huger to Kendall, July 30, 1835.
[33] Letter of 30th, to Kendall.

No man attempted to do his duty in a trying situation more than Huger did. On the same day he wrote to Kendall for instructions, he wrote to his fellow-worker, Postmaster Gouverneur, of the New York City post office, asking that the abolition papers be held until he could hear from the Postmaster-General.[34] The problem would have been effectively solved if the New York postmaster had stopped the papers from being sent out. Huger, on August 5, wrote another letter to the Postmaster-General, this time much along the line which he had written before. He now had consulted the District Attorney and District Judge and they were all of the opinion that Huger had done the correct thing in his method of handling the mail. There could have been no prosecution in the city under any circumstances. All was quiet, and he reminded the Postmaster-General that he anxiously awaited his instructions that he might know whether he was sustained or not by Kendall.[35] The one thing that influenced Huger's action was the fact that he placed the National Government above the state. He felt that at the least provocation the civil authorities of the city would have taken over the operation of the post office.[36] It was to prevent this that Huger had agreed to several compromises. This gives us an idea of the motives which determined his action in this trying time.

The letter from the Postmaster-General was written on August 4, 1835. The interval between the time Huger wrote his letter and the time he received Kendall's letter seemed very long because much had transpired, and there was a decided need of instructions from the Postmaster-General.[37] The first paragraph of the letter was a restatement of what Huger had said. The second paragraph was a consideration of the thing which was of the greatest importance to Huger. Kendall said that upon careful examination of the laws, he was satisfied that the Postmaster-General had no legal authority to exclude newspapers from the mail or to prohibit their carriage or delivery on account of their character or tendency, real or supposed. He was of the opinion that it was not thought wise by Congress to confer upon the head of an executive department power over the press which

[34] Richmond Enquirer, August 25, 1835. Letter of 30th.
[35] Huger to Kendall, August 5, 1835.
[36] Letter from Huger to Kendall, August 5, 1835.
[37] Letter from Kendall to Huger, August 4, 1835. Huger did not have the letter when he wrote on August 5.

might be perverted and abused. In spite of the clear statement of the law as it existed Kendall said that he was not prepared to direct the postmaster at Charleston to deliver the papers. He felt that the post office was created for the benefit of the people and not for their destruction. Kendall said that he had not seen the papers and could not know their character, as none of them had been forwarded to him by Huger. He closed his letter by an appeal to the "Higher Law." "By no act or direction of mine, official or private, could I be induced to aid knowingly in giving circulation to papers of this description, directly or indirectly. We owe an obligation to the laws, but we owe a higher one to the communities in which we live; and if the former be perverted to destroy the latter, it is patriotism to disregard them. Entertaining these views I cannot sanction and will not condemn the steps you have taken. Your justification must be looked for in the character of the papers detained and the circumstances by which you are surrounded."[38]

Huger had every right to expect definite instructions from his superior, the Postmaster-General, in order that he might be relieved of the responsibility which he had taken upon himself. In this he was disappointed, for the reply was an evasive one, yet there is little doubt that as far as the Postmaster-General was concerned the papers were not to be distributed, regardless of either the Federal or the state laws. The postmaster would neither vindicate nor condemn Huger. The letter from Kendall did not reach Huger until August 10, 1835.[39] He hastened to send copies of the abolition papers, that the Postmaster-General might have them before him for his observation. The people, Huger said, were of one accord regardless of party. That Huger was still confused and not helped by the evasive answers is brought out by his letter of August 10. He said, "For myself, I am perfectly willing to let my justification depend upon the character of the papers detained and the circumstances by which I am surrounded." This he had quoted from the Postmaster-General's letter. Then he said, "If it is the direction of the Department that I forward these papers, I must do so; but it will be with my solemn conviction that nothing short of the regular army could protect the mail in which they are contained. The

[38] Letter from Kendall to Huger; *Niles Register*, XLVII, 446.
[39] From Huger to Kendall, August 10, 1835; *Richmond Enquirer*, August 25, 1835.

whole civil, judicial, and military authorities of South Carolina are ready to intercept it. I cannot take upon me to put in peril the immense amount of property which is daily passing through my hands, unless especially ordered to do so."[40]

The situation in Charleston was unusually serious and Huger was trying to meet it. The city council at the request of Huger had furnished nightly a guard to protect the property.[41] The postmaster did not think this was actually necessary but was doing it as a precautionary measure. By August 14, Huger could write the Postmaster-General that all was quiet in Charleston, and he considered the tranquillity and safety of the mail as practically restored.[42] There was a strong feeling of regret in the whole community for the outrage committed upon the post office. He thought also that the letter of the postmaster which had now been published had brought great satisfaction and had done much to promote peace and harmony. These letters give an idea of the confusion and excitement which raged in Charleston and of the method Huger used to handle the situation.

Huger had been helped in the solution of this problem in Charleston by his fellow postmaster, Gouverneur, in New York, to whom he had appealed.[43] Gouverneur took it upon himself to keep the abolition literature out of the mail. He wrote to the president of the American Anti-Slavery Society of New York explaining the letter which had just come to him from his associate in Charleston asking for his coöperation. He asked the society to suspend the transmission of its papers until the Postmaster-General could be heard from.[44] The American Anti-Slavery Society refused to comply with the request and insisted that there could be no such class discrimination. The society demanded the same rights as those granted to other persons and organizations.[45] The New York postmaster expressed surprise that the society did not comply with his request, claiming that

---

[40] Letter of Huger to Kendall, August 10, 1835.

[41] *Richmond Enquirer*, August 25, 1835.

[42] Huger to Kendall.

[43] Huger to Kendall, August 10. This was the second letter of that date. It is not complete in the *Richmond Enquirer*, August 25. Extract is given.

[44] Letter from Gouverneur to American Anti-Slavery Society, August 7, 1835. *Niles Register*, XLVIII, 447.

[45] Letter from the American Anti-Slavery Society to Postmaster Gouverneur of August 8, 1835. Signed by E. Wright, Secretary Domestic Correspondence. Letter from Gouverneur to American Anti-Slavery Society August 9, 1835. *Niles Register*, XLVII, 448.

the society's representative had agreed verbally with Bates, the assistant postmaster of the city, through whom the request concerning the suspension was sent.[46] Whether this contention of the postmaster of New York is correct or not we shall never know, for like so many verbal contests there are no records available. It does not seem reasonable, however, that the society would have agreed to this restriction, as such a restriction would have run counter to the cause of education to which they were devoted and would have forced them to give up rights guaranteed by the Constitution.

It is reasonable to suppose that the postmaster of New York had made up his mind to support his associate in Charleston, no matter what the answer from the society might be. He let the society know that he did not intend to send the papers and that he held himself responsible to the Postmaster-General and to the laws. There was only one way that the abolition society could have had its grievances redressed and that was to resort to the courts. Amos Kendall in speaking of this affair many years later said, "The fact that the abolition societies did not resort to the courts was proof that they were wrong and that the posmasters were acting within their rights."[47] This may be the correct view; but knowing the excitement in the country as the abolitionists must have known it, it is hard to see how they could have expected to aid their cause in any court of justice. They were willing to wait and to arouse public opinion to demand, not that the papers should be sent, but that the freedom of the press be assured.

After Gouverneur's controversy with the Anti-Slavery Society he wrote to Kendall on August 11, asking for instructions and for vindication in holding back the antislavery papers in New York.[48] His answer came from Kendall on August 22, eleven days after his own letter was written to the Postmaster-General. The letter was much longer and more detailed than the one which had been addressed to Huger. The Postmaster-General explained the long delay in answering. The documents which Gouverneur had intended to enclose were overlooked and the Postmaster-General could not answer until he saw them. They were fortu-

[46] *Niles Register*, XLVII, 448.
[47] Amos Kendall, *Autobiography*, 648.
[48] *Niles Register*, XLIX, 8; letter of Kendall to Gouverneur, August 22, 1835. *Ibid.*, XLIX, 8.

nately printed in the papers, and the Postmaster-General did not
need to wait any longer. He explained his own attitude to the
New York postmaster such as he had done for Huger.[49] He
made it clear that if he had the power he would exclude all the
abolition papers from the Southern mails. He went into a long
argument on the nature of the states, as to what they had lost
and what they had kept by the formation of the Union. He
even doubted whether the abolitionist had a right to use the
mails since that use was prohibited by the southern states, and
he insisted that the National Government had no right to send
material which was objected to by them. He did not hesitate
to state his views on the authority of the states to determine
what should be distributed within their borders which after all
is a "States' Rights" argument.[50] The letter to the postmaster
in New York differed from the one to Huger because it made
no plea for the "Higher Law."

The reason this "Higher Law" was not invoked again may
have been because there had been so much criticism of it. The
New York Evening Post argued that a man, like Kendall, who
would advocate that every postmaster was a judge of the laws
and when such laws should be suspended, ought to retire to private life.[51] It asked, "What higher law can we owe to the community than to obey the laws which that community has framed?"
The paper wanted to know who was to decide other than the
community itself what was to be the law.[52] No one knew better
than Kendall that this appeal to the "Higher Law" was weak
and dangerous. His argument was a direct appeal to set aside
laws if they conflicted with the interest of the communities and
the South. This doctrine found few supporters in the North.
The Postmaster-General changed his argument to show that
after all it was the state which must be considered. The difference in the sections of the country probably accounts for the
difference in the wording of the letters. The sentiment in both
is unmistakably that the individual postmaster would determine

[49] Letter of Kendall to Gouverneur, *Ibid.*, 9.
[50] *Richmond Whig and Public Advertiser*, August 21, 1835. Article
quoted from *New York Evening Post*. The *Post* said, however displeasing
the tone of the South is, it is insignificant as compared with the theoretical
violation of Mr. Gouverneur.
[51] *Niles Register*, XLVIII, 448. Extract from the *Post*.
[52] Extracts from a letter from the postmaster at Madison, Georgia, to the
Postmaster-General.

the policy concerning these objectionable papers. The Postmaster-General's convictions were so plain that it seems peculiar he did not order the papers to be held at all hazards.

While Huger and Gouverneur were having their difficulties handling the abolition papers there were other postmasters in difficulty who were appealing to the Postmaster-General for instructions. On July 31, 1835, the postmaster at Madison, Georgia, asked his chief for instructions. The problem which he wanted solved was a very interesting one. The papers, he said, were addressed to persons who were not subscribers and who would not pay the postage and take them out, and thus allowed papers to clutter his office. He could not sell them for postage, as that would aid in the distribution of these papers; and in Georgia he would be sent to the penitentiary for in any way aiding in the distribution of the papers. There were complaints from the assistant postmaster of Richmond, Virginia, also asking for instructions. He had been called upon to stop these papers by leading men of his city.[53] The Raleigh, North Carolina, postmaster asked for instructions, for he did not know what to do with the papers as the persons to whom they were addressed would not take them. There were none addressed to persons of color or of a suspicious character, he told Kendall.[54] The postmaster at Orange Court House, Virginia, had kept the papers but doubted his authority and wrote for confirmation of his action.[55] The postmaster at Norfolk presented a resolution of the Husting Court for the regulation of the papers.[56] The postmaster at Columbia, South Carolina, and Augusta, Georgia, were called upon by leading citizens and asked not to distribute the papers; they too asked for instructions.[57] The Petersburg, Virginia, postmaster sent a set of resolutions which called upon the Postmaster-General to adopt such regulations as would prevent those papers coming to that city.[58] Kendall replied to this letter on August 20, restating what he had already told Huger and Gouverneur,

[53] Edmond Anderson to Amos Kendall, August 3, 1835. *Richmond Enquirer*, August 25, 1835.

[54] Scott to Kendall, August 4, 1835. *Ibid*.

[55] Extracts from letter to postmaster at Orange Court House, August 4, 1835, *Ibid*.

[56] Walter E. Jones to Kendall, August 5, 1835. A copy of the resolution is given in the *Richmond Enquirer*.

[57] Columbia, August 5; D. Faust to Kendall, August 8, 1835, *Richmond Enquirer*.

[58] J. D. Townes to Kendall, August 10, 1835. *Ibid*.

that he possessed no authority to deal with the matter. He said at that time there was no method of dealing with the matter, that it had been left to the responsibility of the postmaster, and he could only hope Congress would work out some plan.[59]

It is not surprising that these papers caused confusion in the post offices, for the question was new. The papers had descended upon the postmasters so suddenly that they did not know what to do with them. They were beset on the one hand with hostile citizens and on the other with lack of instructions from the Postmaster-General. The Postmaster-General by his instructions had left the postmasters in difficulty. He had requests from all sides both from the postmasters and from the papers. The *Richmond Whig* asked for the Postmaster-General's views, and he forwarded a copy of his letter to the postmaster at Charleston.[60] This letter to Huger was written largely for consumption in the South. One writer has called this action of the United States Postmaster-General nullification in that it encouraged public officers to violate the laws they were sworn to uphold.[61]

When this new problem had been presented to Kendall he at once informed President Andrew Jackson. On August 7, three days after he had answered Huger's letter, he wrote to Jackson informing him of the confusion in Charleston and including the letter from Huger and also the one from the Richmond post office. He was convinced, he told Jackson, that the only way that the mail could be secure was through the exclusion of the abolition papers. He had decided that he would exclude them and say as little about it as possible. Kendall further said, it seemed best to him that no orders should be given but that the several postmasters be allowed to act upon such orders as were given in his first letter to the postmaster at Charleston.[62]

We understand why Kendall did not give the order that the

[59] *Niles Register*, XLIX, 8.
[60] *National Intelligencer*, August 12, 1835. Quoted from *Richmond Whig*.
[61] J. W. Burgess, *The Middle Period*, 273. This same view was held by Thomas Williams in *Enemies of the Constitution*. Open letter to the Postmaster-General. A letter had just been published in the *Northern Press* which had been taken from the *Richmond Whig* which asked the postmaster to avow or deny. It was only hoped he would deny the letter, for it did not show Kendall as straightforward as he was supposed to be. He had ordered the postmasters to violate the law by looking at the mail which was denied by law and had made the Postmaster-General by a roundabout way a censor of the press.
[62] *Correspondence of Andrew Jackson.* Letter of Kendall to Jackson, August 7, V, 349.

papers be delivered. He knew the condition and was aware that if he gave no orders the papers probably would not be distributed because it was impossible to deliver them in most of the southern states. He actually gave the order in the Washington postoffice that the papers were to be given out only to such persons as claimed them as actual subscribers.[63] This order was not written but verbal. He closed this letter by expressing the belief that if these steps were carried out, they would pacify the South. He asked the President for his views.

The President replied to this important letter two days later, August 9. He expressed regret that such men as the abolitionists lived in our country and said if they could be caught they ought to be made to atone for their crime with their lives. He said further that we are the instruments and executors of the law, that there was no power to prohibit anything from being transported in the mail if that thing was authorized by law. He approved, moreover, the method that Kendall had used in his verbal message to the Washington postmaster with the addition of taking the names of those subscribers for the papers. He suggested that the names should be published that all might see those who were responsible for aiding the abolition agitation. While Jackson was outspoken against the abolition societies, he regretted the breaking open of the post office at Charleston and the seizure of those inflammatory papers, because he felt sure that a spirit of mob law was becoming too common and had to be checked. Jackson could see that there would be confusion, but directed the papers to be delivered to actual subscribers until Congress met.[64]

The policy of Jackson and Kendall differed in that Kendall would follow a vacillating course while Jackson would follow the law. Jackson could not see that the postmasters should use discretion in the matter; they must deliver the papers while the law remained. This letter came after Jackson's contest over nullification and shows the same stern attitude and respect for law which he had manifested in that episode, while Kendall, desirous of pleasing the South, used a vacillating policy.

Since there was no law which allowed the abolition papers to be held, as both Jackson and Kendall claimed, one naturally

[63] *Correspondence of Andrew Jackson*, V. 359.
[64] J. S. Basset, *Correspondence of Andrew Jackson*, Jackson to Kendall, August 9, V. 360.

wonders why the order was not given to the postmasters that the papers be delivered until Congress could put new laws into operation. The reason for this vacillating policy is found partly in the confusion and excitement which necessitated special care for the welfare of the mail on the one hand and for the political situation on the other. Calhoun and Van Buren were the leaders in the Jacksonian party after the election of 1828. It was doubtful which one would have the support of Jackson; but whichever did secure it would succeed Jackson in 1836. When the question of Jackson's invasion of Florida came before the cabinet in Monroe's administration, Calhoun was for stern measures toward Jackson, for his unauthorized action. It was John Q. Adams who defended him. Jackson always was under the impression that it was Calhoun who defended him. When Jackson ascertained in writing from Crawford that Calhoun stood to the contrary, he demanded an explanation, to which the gentleman gave an evasive answer. On May 13, 1830, Jackson sent Crawford's letter and a curt note to Calhoun for reply.[65] This episode killed whatever chance Calhoun had for the support of Jackson. Shepherd gives the opinion that Jackson had selected Van Buren before this episode started, but certainly by 1832 Van Buren was definitely selected and the President and Calhoun had come to the parting of the ways.[66] No man knew Jackson's wishes better than Kendall. He had been a member of the Kitchen Cabinet from the beginning of Jackson's political career. He was in a position to express the will of the administration.

It was rumored as early as April, 1835, that Kendall would be appointed Postmaster-General and that Barry would be sent as minister to Spain.[67] It was said Kendall was made acting postmaster so that if he were not confirmed by the Senate he would still have his auditorship. Kendall's confirmation being in doubt, he could say nothing that would offend the South. Van Buren was also in the contest for the presidency with one of the favorite sons of the South. Calhoun wanted to discredit Jackson's party, so if he announced a policy which would allow the institutions of the South to be attacked, he would lose votes for the Jacksonian machine, thereby accomplishing his purpose. The motive was political. To say, on the one hand, that the papers

[65] H. Von Holst, *John C. Calhoun*, American Statesman Series, 91.
[66] E. M. Shepherd, *Martin Van Buren*, American Statesman Series, 163.
[67] *Niles Register*, XLVIII, 91.

must be sent would have prevented the confirmation for Kendall which would have been a blow at the administration and would have in all probability lost the South to Van Buren; on the other hand, to say the papers must not be sent would have been destructive to Van Buren in the North.[68] This gives a reason for the rather ambiguous letters which were planned to please all parties concerned. Kendall was a party chief, measuring his expressions in terms of party welfare.

[68] J. Parton, *Life of Andrew Jackson*, III, 587.

CHAPTER III

THE ATTEMPT TO CONTROL ABOLITION PAPERS

The papers which were distributed to the communities of the South brought great excitement in all sections. It was felt to be necessary to find some way to control the matter. The fact that the Postmaster-General had given every postmaster in the South the power to use his own discretion in the distribution of this objectionable literature was not satisfactory. It was deemed necessary to find ways to stop the flow of the papers. The *Richmond Enquirer* thought this was necessary on the part of the South because the citizens of the North did not know the nature of the papers nor the danger they were likely to produce. This paper estimated that not one person in ten thousand in the North had seen one of these papers. The South knew the perils, felt the mischief, and prepared to do all in its power to prevent the invasion of these papers and hinder their publication. In spite of this, it could not prevent all papers from reaching their destination and every effort had to be put forth to arrest them.[1]

One suggestion was made which, it was supposed, would curb the flow of this objectionable literature. The papers could not circulate unless the postage was paid, and if every white man in the South refused to pay the postage, then the papers would be sent back. With the energy of the postmasters and of vigilance committees, the paper would be stopped. One southern paper thought the entire territory below the Mason-Dixon Line was under a debt of gratitude to Gouveneur, postmaster of New York City, for his effort in stopping the papers.[2] These were some of the early efforts which, had they been carried out strictly, might have effectively arrested the literature.

When the papers had reached flood-tide and when excitement was highest, the people looked about for a means of action and

---

[1] *The Philanthropist*, New Richmond, January 8, 1936, quoted from the *Enquirer*.

[2] *Southern Patriot*, August 22, 1835. The action of Gouveneur was important, the *Patriot* thought, because the greater part of the abolition papers came from the North.

resorted to meetings to take counsel. After they had taken the law into their own hands, broken into the post office, and burned the mail in the city of Charleston, the people held a meeting on August 4, which was presided over by the intendant.[3] At this meeting a committee of twenty-one was appointed to examine the question and to report at a later meeting. In the meantime the city council met and passed a resolution on August 11, 1835, that a committee be appointed to meet the mail on its arrival from New York and elsewhere, see that the mail was conducted to the post office, and examine it under the supervision of the postmaster. The committee was Seymour, Bryan, Graves, Margrath, Henry, and the intendant, with the intendant as chairman. It was the business of this committee to meet every mail, accompany it to the post office, make arrangements with the postmaster, and see that none of the objectionable literature was disturbed. This arrangement John Q. Adams calls the seizure of the mail by a mob of southern gentlemen in cooperation with the postmaster.[4]

The committee of twenty-one made its report on August 11 in the city hall. In the preamble the committee stated it would make no labored argument on the subject of slavery not because it could not be maintained on moral grounds, but because the people of the South intended to have no discussion of the right of slavery in their borders. These rights the states had from the very existence of the colonies, and they were inherent and inalienable.[5] The committee presented a list of twelve resolutions which covered the whole field of slavery. Slavery, according to these resolutions, was a question which belonged exclusively to the states of the Union, and any interference from any other source was inconsistent with the Federal Compact and could not be submitted to. The incendiary societies must be looked upon with the utmost indignation; they were only calculated to destroy those persons they pretended to help. The fact that there were two hundred and fifty societies in thirteen states and 25,000 to 50,000 copies of these papers which burdened the southern mail showed that there was a necessity for prompt action. The post office could not be made a means of the destruction of the people, because it had been founded for their welfare. It was thought that all that

[3] T. D. Jervey, *Robert Haynes and His Times*, 379.
[4] John Q. Adams, Memoirs, I, 257. *Citizen of Charleston*, 6.
[5] *Citizen of Charleston*. A pamphlet of all the pro-slavery activities in the city of Charleston, 18.

was necessary was for Congress to pass such a law as would make it unlawful for papers to circulate through the states where such circulation was unlawful by the state laws. The real sentiment of this meeting came out when the resolution said its purpose was to let the non-slave states know the feeling of the South. This Charleston meeting thought a better method to meet the situation was by mutual coöperation between these states with common interest. They must unite as one man in a fixed and unalterable determination to maintain their rights and defend their property.[6] Many of these resolutions were sent far and wide.

As Charleston had done, so did Macon, Georgia. Citizens held a meeting early in September, on the call of the mayor, for the purpose of dealing with the antislavery papers. The citizens passed a set of resolutions which stated that the discussion of slavery could cause no other result than irritation.[7]

Beaufort, South Carolina, held a meeting in August for the purpose of dealing with the papers. The meeting was a large one and was presided over by Judge Lynch, of that city.[8]

The citizens of Richmond held a similar meeting to cope with the new problem before them. The subject had been intensified by the action of Charleston. A committee of thirteen was appointed to study the situation and report to a call meeting on August 4.[9] The citizens convened on August 4, and the committee presented a long preamble and a list of resolutions setting forth the attitude of Richmond and Henrico County toward the antislavery papers. The preamble said that when the antislavery society was small it was ignored, but recent developments had shown that the South must exert itself. The question of slavery could not be discussed, for the southern people would not tolerate such glaring, iniquitous arguments. The resolutions, much after the fashion of those in Charleston, asked for a vigilance committee and an amendment of the laws, if they were not sufficient to prevent the circulation of antislavery literature.[10] The Richmond meeting registered its opposition to the societies when the flood of papers first started.

The meetings were held all over the South for the purpose

[6] *Niles Register*, XLVIII, 447. *Citizens of Charleston*, edited by the Vigilance Committee, Documents of Charleston, S. C.

[7] *Savannah Republican*, September 7, 1835.

[8] *Richmond Enquirer*, September 1, 1835. The meeting was held on Saturday, August 15.

[9] *Niles Register*, XLVIII, 400.

[10] *Ibid.*, 144.

of arresting the matter. The meeting at Louisa, Virginia, passed a set of resolutions pledging its support to the postmasters who should keep objectionable papers. Those who refused to keep the papers were to be condemned as accomplices of the crime and to be subject to popular indignation. The meeting instructed James Garland from that District and the other representatives from the South to vacate their seats if Congress should attempt to consider or discuss slavery and to remain away from their seats until such discussion should cease.[11]

There was also a meeting held at Settersburg, Glynn County, Georgia, in August for the purpose of expressing the opinion of that city on this question. This meeting considered the right to hold slaves one of the reserved rights guaranteed when the Constitution was made. The citizens of that county would join with the sister states in whatever means they should adopt to control the situation.[12]

The gathering at Barnville District, South Carolina, passed a set of resolutions asking the North to make laws to restrain the abolitionists. The resolution stated that if laws were not made, the South must look to its own welfare.[13] A convention held in McIntosh County, Georgia, approved the work of the Postmaster-General and of the postmasters of New York and Charleston. The resolutions went further and condemned the ministers for the part they had played in this controversy.[14] Indignant citizens at the meetings expected the ministers of the various denominations to express their condemnation of the abolitionist. The meeting held at Wilmington, North Carolina, was ready to thank the people of Charleston for their patriotic action.[15] During this same period a gathering was held in Jacksonboro, Screven County, Georgia. A vigilance committee was appointed at this assemblage to confer with the postmaster of that place in order to protect the use of the mails and drive out abolition papers.[16]

[11] New York American, September 9, 1835, quoted from Richmond Enquirer.
[12] Savannah Republican, September 4, 1835.
[13] The Philanthropist, January 15, 1836. Resolution of the 16th section; the vigilance committee was to: (1) confer with the postmasters within its limits, (2) seize upon and have burned all incendiary papers, (3) see that the laws were enforced, (4) keep an eye on all suspicious characters, (5) promptly bring persons to justice, (6) take care of the community against incendiaries.
[14] Savannah Republican, September 9, 1835.
[15] Southern Patriot, September 1, 1835.
[16] Savannah Republican, September 21, 1835.

It can be seen that the whole South was making an effort to deal with the papers which were reaching them. The meetings were by no means confined to the large cities, but were in all parts of the South. This was a new problem which the South had to face, and it was only natural that the southern citizens should discuss such a problem in meetings like those mentioned above. Another illustration of southern feeling may be found in the fact that the town meetings in that section were serving notice on the northern states to stop this literature.

While the South was holding meetings in order to solve its problem, the North was also holding gatherings in various places to solve the problem of abolition literature. These meetings were held in the large cities of the North. One of the largest slave gatherings was held in New York in August. This assemblage was made up of every class of society. The citizens deplored slavery and all its attending evils but could not approve of the wholesale condemnations of the southern people and those of the North who had relation with the slaveholders. According to the preamble the majority of the people of the North did not believe in the immediate abolition of slavery.[17] The resolutions maintained the right of private judgement and free discussion on the slavery issue as on all other questions, but did not think that the North had a right to interfere with slavery. The idea of immediate abolition was grounded upon error. This convention did not believe in giving up its rights as guaranteed by the Constitution but insisted that slavery was a local matter.

An assemblage was held in Utica, New York, in the early part of September for the purpose of arresting the action of the abolitionists. The resolutions held that those who circulated these papers among the slaves were virtually guilty of a breach of the Constitutional compact and were at war with the highest obligation of humanity and justice. This could only have the effect of exciting a spirit of revolt and would bring on a servile war. This meeting expressed the opinion that it was the duty of the North to oppose the abolitionists in every way possible, especially by public gatherings and by the press.[18] The meeting in Philadelphia was held in Music Hall in compliance with a demand of the southern states. The citizens in this assemblage said what

[17] *Niles Register*, XLIX, 9. This meeting was attended by some of the leading people of the city.
[18] *New York American*, September 12, 1835.

the citizens had said in all the other meetings, that measures must be found to arrest the distribution of these papers. However, if there had been a revolt of the slaves, the young men of the North would have joined with the South in putting it down. The legislature of Pennsylvania was called upon to pass such legislation as would protect the South.[19]

A convention was held in the city of Boston on August 3, to show New England's attitude toward this recent excitement. This conference, held in Faneuil Hall, was attended by the most influential people of that city.[20] This gathering passed a resolution to leave to the states the relation of master and slave, and condemned all attempts to appeal to slaves against their masters.[21] There was another large meeting held in Faneuil Hall on August 22, and attended by the most respectable citizens of Boston.[22] The gathering was addressed by many, among whom was Harrison Gray Otis. He was a very old man and took part in this meeting only because, like Calhoun when Mason read his address before Congress on the Compromise of 1850, he thought he owed it to his country to exert his last effort to prevent disunion. He was sure disunion would be the result unless every effort was made to control the situation. He thought the very fact that the abolition societies did not address the papers to the slaves was an indication that abolitionists felt they were wrong.[23] The citizens at this assemblage said in their resolutions that slavery found no place among them, but they did not attempt to force others to think as they did. They also condemned all organizations that attempted to operate in the slave states without the consent of those states.[24] There was an anti-abolition gathering held at Town Hall, in Cambridge, Massachusetts, on September 9. It did not purpose to discuss slavery morally or politically, for the National Government by its Constitution had left to the states all power not delegated to the National Government. This was one of the things which had been left to the state. The citizens had used language not demanded by the occasion, but would not deny the

[19] *Ibid.*, August 26, 1835.
[20] H. H. Hilary, *Abolition Crusade*, 64.
[21] H. H. Hilary, *Abolition Crusade*, 65.
[22] *Boston Advertiser and Patriot*, August 22, 1835. This meeting was attended by such persons as Harrison Gray Otis and Theodore Lyman, Jr., mayor of the city.
[23] *Niles Register*, XLIX, 11.
[24] *Boston Advertiser*, August 22, 1835.

freedom of speech and the right of discussion.[25]   It can be seen that Boston was just as determined as any other city to put a stop to these papers and bring peace to the country.

There were other sections of New England determined to express their opinion on this matter.   The town of Portsmouth, New Hampshire, held a meeting to express its disapproval of the abolition societies and to show its sympathy for the good people of the southern states.   The citizens of that city insisted that slavery was a concern of the South and that section alone; it needed no assistance from the abolition societies.   The circulation of the papers was considered a death blow to the Union.[26]   New Haven also held such a meeting in response to the request from Charleston.   It was attended by the best people of the town.   This conference condemned the circulation of the papers because they were meddling with a right which belonged exclusively to the South.[27]

There took place at this time a gathering at Bangor, Maine, in order to show its sympathy for the South; the papers were incendiary and should be suppressed.   This meeting expressed the idea that it was shameful and was an abuse of the freedom of the press for the North to allow such papers as *Human Rights, The Emancipator,* or *The Liberator* to be sent to the southern people.[28]

It can be seen that in order to cope with the flood of anti-slavery literature meetings were being held in both sections.   The South had called them as the first means of handling the antislavery papers.   They were also called to appeal to the northern communities and states to stop the abolition publications. The North, while it condemned the abolition societies, would not destroy the freedom of speech or of the press.   The meetings were called largely at the suggestion of the southern cities.   The northern assemblages were held in the large cities.   In the South they were held in the rural sections as well as in the cities.   The meetings tended to show the attitude of the people in both the North and the South.

While the assemblages were attempting to handle these papers in an orderly manner, certain groups decided to handle the mat-

[25] *New York American,* September 14, 1835.
[26] *Boston Advertiser,* September 9, 1835.
[27] Steiner, *Slavery in Connecticut,* 74.
[28] *New York American,* September 12, 1835.

ter in their own way.[29] One paper thought that the advocates of immediate abolition had a great deal for which to answer; for they had succeeded in exciting the communities, sundering the ties which bound man and man together, and loosening the bonds of the Union.[30] This state of affairs grew out of the insurrection of 1831. As a result of this effort, traveling in the South was almost impossible, so wrought up were the people of that section. This statement came from a gentleman (he did not give his name) who was traveling in Georgia in 1835.[31] James Otis, a lawyer of Portland, Maine, and co-editor of the *Portland Advertiser,* narrowly escaped lynching in the town of Lynchburg, Virginia, because he expressed the opinion that, in spite of the money offered, the South did not want Tappan. Tappan was wanted at the South in several places and large rewards were offered for him. Otis escaped only because he allowed his baggage to be searched.[32] In Halifax County, Virginia, a man named David F. Robertson, a Scottish teacher, was in danger of his life because another man named Robertson was suspected of having dropped a copy of *Human Rights* on a steamboat.[33]

The attitude of the South was shown in another way in this same year. The Reverend Amos Dresser, a young theological student, left Cincinnati for the South July 1, 1835, for the purpose of selling books. He made the mistake of wrapping some of his books with antislavery papers. When he got to Nashville his carriage needed mending. This he had done, but overlooked some of the antislavery papers which covered his books. He was reported to the vigilance committee, given trial, and found guilty; the papers served as witness against him. Dresser was given twenty lashes and was glad to escape with that.[34]

[29] *Cincinnati Daily Gazette,* June 2, 1835.

[30] *Cincinnati Daily Gazette,* June 2, 1832.

[31] *Savannah Republican,* September 21, 1835.

[32] *New York American,* September 9, 1835. When suspicion fell on him, he had to do much talking to convince the people of Lynchburg that he was not delivering the papers.

Richmond Enquirer, August 4, 1835. The South, this paper thought, should keep an eye on all suspicious strangers. There were only two ways that these papers could reach the South—one was by emissaries and the other by public mail. The vigilance committee would take care of the emissaries. Woe unto those who should be caught. The control of the mail was another matter. How far the postmaster could go was not known.

[33] *Memoirs of John Q. Adams,* IX, 257.

[34] *Ohio Archaeological and Historical Society,* XX, 1-2, 281. He lost both his vehicle and books, for he did not wait until they were sold.

The relation of whites and Negroes was watched with great care during this period of excitement. Negroes in the mining business in Lumpkin County, Georgia, were accused of association with a group of whites who had no visible means of support. The vigilance committee was ordered by a meeting held on August 22, at Dahlonega to investigate and find out if those whites were distributing antislavery papers among the Negroes.[35] If such persons were found guilty they were to be hanged without waiting for the slow-moving due process of law. The committee was to take the law into its own hands. Three white men were killed around Aiken, South Carolina, and in Jefferson County, Georgia, for the unpardonable crime of associating with Negroes.[36]

Free Negroes were also watched with much vigilance, and every movement was noted with care. There was in the post office at Charleston, South Carolina, a letter addressed to a Negro. He did not come for it but sent a white man with the order. The latter was refused. The post office took this opportunity to open the letter.[37] It did contain some information which was interpreted as endorsing insurrection. Another case, which showed how determined the vigilance committee was to observe the movement of free Negroes, came later. Two Negroes, Parker and Williams, came to Mobile early in September, 1836. With them were their wives. They were arrested, and their baggage was searched. In Parker's baggage was found a few numbers of the *Struggler*, a paper printed by Negroes in Philadelphia.[38] Parker was examined and sent to prison. Although he did have antislavery papers, his punishment was much lighter than it would have been had those papers been branded by the South as incendiary.

The South was determined that it would control those persons who traveled in its territory. It is a mistake to suppose that the papers reached the South only by the mails, they often found their way otherwise, and the South knew it. The South placed every visitor from the North under suspicion. Not every one received the treatment which has been noted above, but all were under suspicion.

[35] *Savannah Republican*, September 9, 1835.
[36] *The Southern Patriot*, September 11, 1835.
[37] *Ibid.*, August 30, 1835.
[38] *Mobile Register*, September 7, 1836. This paper is one of the unknown ones. It is difficult to find it; its nature is doubtful.

In spite of the treatment which had been administered to some who had visited the South, there was a feeling that a stop could be put to this whole thing if the leaders could be brought below the Mason Dixon Line. The *Alexandria Gazette* extended invitations to Garrison, Tappan, and Thompson to visit the South. They were asked to visit any place south of the Potomac and they were guaranteed a warm reception.[39]   Thompson was very much wanted because some blamed him for a great deal of anti-slavery excitement.[40]   His presence in the United States was resented because he was from Great Britain and his language was considered rash.

In the city of Macon it was said by the *Macon Messenger* that $12,000 had been raised for the delivery of Arthur Tappan within the limits of the state.[41]   The town of Aiken, South Carolina, in its anti-abolition meeting in early September passed a set of resolutions; one of these resolutions offered $1,000 for the detection of any one attempting to distribute antislavery literature or interfere in any way with southern rights.[42]   The vigilance committee of the Parish of Prince William, South Carolina, offered a reward of $1,000 for the detection and delivery of any-one who should be proven to have been an active agent in the service of the antislavery society.[43]   The cities and the vigilance committee were active because they felt that this method would keep the abolitionists out, and those who came would be more easily detected.

There was overheard a conversation in New York City indicating that a plot was on to abduct Arthur Tappan, a prominent abolitionist. It was further rumored that there was a fund of $20,000 for the purpose of rewarding those who should deliver these persons to the South.[44]   The *New York American* thought it nonsense that Tappan should be menaced with kidnapping. The *Richmond Whig* did not hold the same view; it felt that the scoundrel who had set a whole country in flames, tightened the discipline upon two million people, and subjected innocent men

[39] Quoted by the *Savannah Republican*, August 10, 1835.
[40] C. G. Bowers, *The Party Battles of the Jackson Period.*
[41] *Savannah Republican*, September 7, 1835.   The paper spoke of him as a bloodhound abolitionist.
[42] *Southern Patriot*, September 12, 1835.
[43] *Daily Advertiser and Patriot*, August 21, 1835, quoted from *Southern Patriot*.   It was rumored that there was an abolition agent around Beaufort.
[44] *Savannah Republican*, September 11, 1835.   The *New York Herald* said it did not like the abolitionists but was giving them fair warning.

to the lash ought not to enjoy unmolested security.[45]   The *American* said if Tappan was guilty of what he was accused by the *Whig* the law would reach him; if not the *Whig* might rest assured that there were arms enough to protect him, though all Virginia should be aiding in the kidnapping.[46]

The citizens of Glynn County, Georgia, were ready to handle the matter in quite a different way.   They would request Governor Lumpkin to call upon the President of the United States for the arrest and trial of Garrison, Thompson, Tappan, Cornish Cox, Rankin, Leavitt, Goodell, and Wright for an attempt to incite insurrection and domestic violence.   The resolution held that this could be done under the fourth article of the Constitution of the United States[47]

They further gave the governor an alternative method, viz: if the President should decline the request, he was to proclaim an offer of $5,000 appropriated by the joint resolution of the Legislature of 1831 to bring to justice enemies of the peace and safety of the South.[48]   Three men were wanted by all means at the South, for it was believed that the abolition papers could be stopped if only a few of the leaders could be brought to justice. It would have been a dangerous precedent to allow any state the power to extradite citizens from one state to another, regardless of the crime, if the person had never been to that state.

The southern states felt that the one way to put an end to these objectionable periodicals was for the North to extradite the leaders of this movement to the South.   These leaders would be charged with criminal offenses, an idea advocated by the *Milledgeville Times*.   This journal argued that, if the act committed was a crime in the southern states, the offender might be transported.[49] Alabama was the first state to try out this rather novel method advocated by the *Milledgeville Times*.   The Grand Jury of Tuscaloosa County indicted R. G. Williams for inciting the slaves against their masters and demanded his extradition from the state

[45] *New York American*, September 15, 1835.
[46] *Ibid.*, Editorial.
[47] The particular section in question is Section 4, Article 2.   That part which deals with fugitives from justice reads: "A person charged in any state with treason, felony or other crime, who shall flee from justice and be found in another state, shall on demand of the executive authority of the state from which he fled, be delivered up to be removed to the state having jurisdiction of the crime."
[48] *Savannah Republican*, September 14, 1835.
[49] *Richmond Whig*, August 14, 1835, quoted from the *Milledgeville Times*.

of New York. Williams had said, "God commands, and all nature cries out, that man should not be held as property. The system of making man property has plunged 2,250,000 of our fellow countrymen into the deepest physical and moral degradation, and they are every moment sinking deeper."[50] Armed with this indictment, Governor Gayle, of Alabama, made a requisition upon Governor Marcy, of New York, for the extradition of Williams. The southern Governor made the demand in the usual form, resting his case upon the law of the United States with respect to fugitives and persons escaping from justice. The indictment stated plainly that Williams was a fugitive from justice, and therefore was wanted for crimes which he had committed in Alabama. The truth came out in the letter which Governor Gayle wrote to Governor Marcy, of New York. In this letter he admitted that Williams had not been in the state, but inasmuch as the papers which he published had stirred up sedition in Alabama he was a fugitive from justice.[51] This is a strange case; the Governor admitted that Williams had not been in the state, yet the indictment names the day when he stirred up sedition. Gayle, in his message to his own legislature, insisted that it was a mistake to apply the rule of strict construction to all parts of the Constitution. Some parts, he thought, should be interpreted liberally, while others should be interpreted literally. Just how the Governor would decide which sections should be interpreted liberally and which strictly is difficult to say.

The Governor of New York was forced to differ from the Governor of Alabama with reference to the precedent which he was asked to set.[52] Williams, he said, as the indignant chief executive of the aggrieved state admitted, had never been in the state of Alabama and could not be considered a fugitive from justice.[53] Marcy, in his reply, entered into a long discussion of the nature of the Constitution and the amendments thereto. He closed with the only answer he could possibly give, a definite refusal to return Williams.

[50] *Niles Register*, XLIX, 353. Taken from a copy of the indictment which Governor Marcy presented to the New York Legislature.
[51] *National Intelligencer*, February 14, 1835. All documents dealing with the case are not to be found in *Niles Register*, XLIX, 359.
[52] Reply of Governor Marcy to Governor Gayle, December 8, 1835. *Niles Register*, XLIX, 359.
[53] From Gayle's letter of November 14, 1835, and from extracts of his message to the Legislature of Alabama. *Niles Register*, XLIX, 358-359.

This was one method, it was thought, by which the abolition leaders could be reached. Everyone did not agree, however. The South was not unanimous as to the method which should be used to deal with the matter. A mechanic, writing anonymously in the *Richmond Whig*, said that he could see no value or advantage in bringing Tappan or Garrison to the South, for the Government would be forced to protect them from mob violence and would see that they had a fair trial.[54] Then, furthermore, the maximum punishment that the state could inflict upon these trouble-makers, after all its effort to bring them to trial, was one year's imprisonment, and of course, that would not stop the evil. The writer suggested some other method be found to punish these persons.

To the contrary also was Hugh S. Legare, who from Brussels wrote Alfred Huger on November 21, 1835, declaring it was wrong for the South to suppose that Tappan and the other leaders might be surrendered. The northern people dared not give up these men. Such action would not be suffered, he said, and if it were suffered, it would do more harm than good to the South, for it would put that section in the wrong light. Such extreme actions as some in the South asked for, he felt, would embitter the good men of all nations under the sun against the South. He asked that they do no more than wait on the action of Congress.[55] The reason he would have the South halt in her action and depend upon the regular order of law was that it was the only means of salvation.

When Williams could not be reached by indictments, threats were sent to him along with the return of the papers. Such a letter was sent to him from the Mt. Clio post office, Sumter District, South Carolina, informing him that the paper which he published had been sent back with a knife, a goose with some cotton yarn in its mouth, and some other products of the South. If by any means he did not understand, he might call at the Mt. Clio post office for a practical demonstration.[56] Another let-

[54] *Richmond Whig*, October 9, 1835. The article was signed simply "Mechanic."

[55] *Legare Writings*, Vol. I, 223. Letter from Hugh S. Legare to Alfred Huger at Charleston.

[56] *Richmond Enquirer*, September 1, 1835.
Mt. Clio, August 12, 1835.
Mr. R. G. Williams:
Sir, inclosed paper published by you for the anti-slavery Society, and sent to the Mt. Clio post office, Sumter District, South Carolina, called *Human Rights*, and as no person requested it I now take the liberty of sending it

ter was sent to Williams from Georgetown much in the same tone. It said the writer was returning his paper because he refused to have such a paper around as it had all the earmarks of treason. Williams was asked why he and his friends did not come out in the open instead of working in the dark. The writer chided the New York editor for being afraid of Judge Lynch and closed by saying he desired to see one of those abolitionists in that section, for there were many rope factories out of work.[57] The attitude toward these papers and Williams caused at least one subscriber to cancel his subscription to the *New York American*. This slave owner said that he had taught his slave to read and it was a calamity. The *American* was much too liberal and insisted upon discussing the question of slavery. The way this subscriber would keep the discussion away from the slave was to do away with the papers.[58] These letters were threats and could be useful only if leaders were captured; and since the leaders could not be captured all this might be lost.

There was another method suggested, that of non-importation agreements. The *Southern Patriot* called attention of southern merchants to the justice and propriety of extending trade to those cities of the North which had complied with the request of the South and suggested forming non-importation agreements against the others.[59] This was one method, it was thought, which would bring the North to a realization of the importance of this situation. Some sections were determined to use this as a means of influencing public opinion. A meeting held in McIntosh County, Georgia, took up the matter along with other phases of the antislavery question; it condemned anyone who carried on trade with Tappan or any merchant who should hold Tappan's principles.[60] The mayor of Macon, Georgia, called a meeting at which resolutions were passed to close commercial intercourse with the northern cities unless they came to terms and put down

back, not as it came to this office but embellished on the inside with a knife and on the outside with a goose, with a piece of cotton yarn and all the products of the South. Should you not understand their purpose and use, you can obtain practical information by calling at the Mt. Clio post office. The papers subscribed for and taken at Mt. Clio post office are State right papers and knowing our rights we intend to defend them at all risk and hazards. Postmaster, Mt. Clio.

[57] *Anti-Slavery Record*, September, 1835, Vol. I, No. 9.
[58] *New York American*, October 8, 1835. This subscriber was from Tennessee.
[59] *Niles Register*, XLIX, 74.
[60] *Savannah Republican*, September 9, 1835.

abolition.[61] This was early in September, much too early to know the great response that came from the meetings in the North in their condemnation of the abolitionists.

The *Southern Patriot,* speaking editorially, served notice upon the North that if it wished to keep the trade of the South it must dam up the flood of mischief.[62] Four days later it could report that the merchants of the city of Charleston had met on the third of August for the purpose of taking some action on trade relations with the North. It also hoped to influence other slaveholding states to do likewise. This action the merchants looked upon as a patriotic duty which they owed to their states. They would not trade with the abolitionists or those who condemned them.[63]

The Anti-Abolition Society of Cincinnati wrote a letter to a merchant of that city stating that it had been rumored he was an abolitionist. They asked for his answer which he was to give by placing in the window a card bearing either the word "yes" or "no." Whether he complied or not was not ascertained.[64] A merchant who had a store in both New York and Charleston was informed that if it were proved that he associated with Tappan or John Rankin his Charleston store would be burned.[65] Probably he did not associate with the forbidden characters, for no evidence was unearthed of the burning of the store.

To what extent such threats were carried out and to what extent commerce was influenced is difficult to say. It is very evident that this threat could not have been carried out to the fullest extent, for the South long before this time had become principally a one-crop section, and that crop was cotton. It must get its necessities from other sections and especially from the North and West. The products which the North produced increased every year from 1830 to 1860. One product alone will give some idea. In 1832, 221,000 barrels of flour were sold to New Orleans; by 1847 about 1,618,000 barrels were being sold in the same city.[66] There is a probability that the leading abolitionists felt the boy-

[61] *Ibid.,* September 7, 1835.
[62] July 25, 1835.
[63] *Southern Patriot,* August 4, 1835.
[64] *The Emancipator,* August 11, 1836. This came from the *Emancipator* and may be an extreme case.
[65] Lewis Tappan, *Life of Arthur Tappan,* 244. Evidence might have been overlooked or not reported.
[66] Johnson, E. R., and others, *History of Domestic and Foreign Commerce.* This flour was not for New Orleans but was shipped to all parts of the South.

cott, but it is very evident that there was little interruption of the general trade. The southern meetings did not advocate absolute commercial independence because that was not feasible, but only a boycott on those cities which did not respond. This threat, no doubt, had some influence on the anti-slavery meetings in the North; but it cannot be told exactly how much, for most of the northern meetings responded to the request of the South and condemned the abolitionists. It is reasonable to say that the commercial boycott was not wholly effective and like the other efforts could not stop completely the flow of the papers.

The *Mobile Register* expressed what was considered the view of the South when it said the law should be strengthened and increased in its rigors; and at the same time the springs of domestic government should be braced so as to resist all outside pressure; when this was done, if the law was defective or slow in its movement, then the people should find a remedy in their own strong arms. The remedy to be used was a peaceful and lawful way—if ever there can be such a thing when people take the law in their own hands—force would be used if necessary.[67] The abolitionists had to be kept out of the South and their papers banished from the land. The *Mobile Register* admitted that the language which it used was plain, but justified itself by saying that truth was best understood in that manner.[68] This plain speaking was justified on the ground that the sooner this program was known abroad the better it would be for the peace of the common country. This then explains why so many efforts were made to check the flow of this objectionable literature to the South.

[67] *Mobile Register*, August 10, 1835.
[68] This was not only the wish of the *Register*, but the wish of every southern man, we are informed in this article.

CHAPTER IV

THE CONTEST BETWEEN THE STATES

In spite of the effort put forth by the different citizens to stop the abolition papers, the success was not as satisfactory as one might have expected. There was still a clamor for a better method of controlling this literature. The *Richmond Whig* advocated the setting up of laws by the northern states as the best means of solving the perplexing problem. The editor expressed the opinion that not only did the North owe this to the South, but the South had every right to expect it. He was sure that Massachusetts, New York, and Pennsylvania could fetter these troublesome tongues, but whether or not they would do it was the real question.[1] The methods which the South had employed up to this time could work only if the abolitionists appeared in the South. However, the abolitionists took care not to appear there. The northern states could solve the problem if they would pass laws which would check the flow of this literature and effectively control this group of people who sought to destroy slavery and interfere with the institutions of the South.

The *Southern Patriot* thought the editor of the *Whig* had struck the right chord. The North had no alternative; it must pass such laws as the South called for or else Judge Lynch would preside.[2] This paper pointed out clearly what might be expected in the South. It is difficult to understand what is meant by the threat of the *Southern Patriot*. How these persons could be brought to the South had not been made clear. The resolutions which were passed by the meeting held in Charleston on August 3 express this same idea. The South had a claim upon the non-slaveholding states for the enactment of such laws as would repress abolition papers.[3] The only way that the papers could be stopped legally at that time was for the northern states to do it. The North could have shown that it had no part in the affair by

---

[1] *Editorial*, August 7, 1835.
[2] August 4, 1835.
[3] *Niles Register*, XLVIII, 445; *Richmond Enquirer*, August 7, 1835.

passing such laws as the South demanded.[4] The *Enquirer* thought
it was a question of how far the state could legally go in handling
this question.[5] It was believed in some quarters that the matter
might be controlled by the police power of the state. It is clear
there existed a feeling abroad that the North could be called upon
for laws.

The governors of the various southern states carried out the
suggestions of the papers and the meetings. Some of these governors had not read the *Richmond Whig;* however, they had been
guided by public opinion as the papers had, and had called upon
the North for legislation against these deluded people. The
southern states took up the matter when their legislatures met.
First they called upon the northern states for laws; secondly, they
strengthened their own laws; and thirdly, they sent resolutions to
Congress. The effort to control the abolition papers had passed
now to the legal phase.

Governor McDuffie of South Carolina, in his message to the
legislature of his state, demanded that the individual legislatures
of the northern states should enact laws against incendiary literature about which the South complained.[6] Statesmen and officials
of the northern states had expressed their sympathy for the South
and shown their contempt for the abolitionist, as the popular assemblies and meetings had already done. This McDuffie did not
consider enough, and thus he urged the legislatures of these
northern states to go on record as guaranteeing permanently the
welfare and safety of the southern states. He argued further
that these laws ought to be passed because these papers were published by a band of fanatics in the northern and middle states who
attacked the domestic institution of the South.[7] Penal laws were
demanded as a basis of permanent protection in the name of international law. McDuffie spoke of the states as though they were
nations. His whole argument was based upon ''States' Rights.''

The State Legislature of South Carolina responded to the
request of its governor and appointed a joint committee on Federal relations to which was referred that part of the Governor's
message dealing with incendiary publications. The committee in-

    [4] *Southern Patriot*, July 30, 1835.
    [5] *Richmond Enquirer*, July 31, 1835.
    [6] *American History Leaflet*, No. 10, 12, edited by A. B. Hart. *Southern
Patriot*, November 27, 1835.
    [7] *Richmond Enquirer*, January 1, 1836.

sisted that slavery was purely a state matter and could not be interfered with by either the other states or the National Government.[8] The resolutions followed the reasoning in Governor McDuffie's message that it was the duty of the northern states to pass the legislation demanded. These resolutions were very broad and covered not only incendiary literature but also the petitions for the abolition of slavery in the District of Columbia. These resolutions approved the method which had been used by Post-master-General Kendall to handle the anti-slavery papers. The resolutions stated in threatening and specific language that, even though South Carolina was calling upon the non-slaveholding states for help in this matter, if they did not respond she was still in a position to take care of herself.[9] This was, at least, a broad hint that South Carolina would take it upon herself to protect her institutions to the point of secession.[10] After the committee on Federal relations had made its report, both houses of the legislature passed resolutions which were along the same line as the report of the committee.[11] The resolutions did not carry the threatening section which the report had. These resolutions were just as specific as the report and demanded legislation from the North.

When the Virginia Legislature met in December, 1835, Governor Tazwell gave a labored ''States' Rights'' argument and called upon the legislature for laws to prevent the abolition activities.[12] The legislature of Virginia, like that of South Carolina, responded to the request of the Governor and passed a set of resolutions. The resolutions of Virginia demanded prompt and efficient legislation for the control of those deluded persons in the borders of the northern states who sought to stir up insurrection by the distribution of their seditious papers.[13] Virginia demanded this upon the principle of International Law, which after all applied to every state of the American Union. The legislature gave warning that the control of the slaves in the Commonwealth of

[8] *Niles Register*, XLIX, 318.
[9] *Ibid.*, 319. This sentiment is expressed in the last paragraph of the report of the committee on Federal legislation.
[10] *Ibid.*, 309. The Governor was directed to send a copy to the northern states.
[11] *Niles Register*, XLIX, 309. The Governor was directed to send a copy to the northern states.
[12] *Richmond Enquirer*, December 7, 1835. He was governor of the state from 1834-36.
[13] *Laws of Virginia*, 1835-36, 395.

Virginia belonged exclusively to that state, and that this control must be maintained at all hazards.[14] The resolution set forth the view that any interference with slaves in the southern states was a violation of the Constitution and the Social Compact. These resolutions were to be sent to each representative and senator from the state and a copy to each of the northern states with a request that the resolutions be placed before their legislatures.

The message of Governor Wilson Lumkin of Georgia said the South could hear no argument on the question of slavery, and would allow no intermeddling from outsiders. The duty of those states where the papers were published was specific and clear. It was their duty, as he saw it, to pass such laws against the abolitionist as would protect the South.[15] The new Governor, William Schley, in his inaugural address, called attention to this same evil and asked the North for laws. The North could do this, he thought, if it had the regard and the interest for the South it professed. The North could best stop the abolitionists, he felt, for they were daily under the eyes of the northern people; and it was for them to devise and apply a remedy.[16] It was for the North alone to stop the tide of discontent which was rolling and swelling from the Potomac to the Gulf. This plea from both of the governors was answered by the legislature that same year with a preamble and a set of resolutions. The preamble gave generally the same argument which the governors had advanced. The legislature, familiar with its own law and that of the United States, declared in its first resolution for the freedom of the press, but emphasized the fact that it must not be abused.[17] Whether or not the freedom of the press was abused depended upon whether it attacked the institutions of the South, from the point of view of the legislature. The blessings and security which the Constitution guaranteed to all could be assured only if the letter of the law was observed. The committee became belligerent and said it would suffer no power on earth to interfere with its institutions.[18] But the committee was not unmindful of the fine spirit of co-operation which had been shown by the resolutions of recent meet-

[14] *Niles Register*, XLIX, B-2; Senate Document 233, 24 Congress, 1 Sess.
[15] *Savannah Republican*, November 7, 1835.
[16] *Niles Register*, XLIX, 187.
[17] *Laws of Georgia*, 1834-35, 299. This became a law December 22, 1835.
[18] Resolutions of the Legislature of Georgia, Senate Resolution, Laws of Georgia, 1834-35, 299.

ings at the North and accordingly expressed its appreciation.[19] These resolutions were to be sent to the President of the United States, to the governors of the various states, and to the senators in Congress from the state of Georgia.

Governor Swain of North Carolina, in his annual message, called the attention of the legislature of his state to the northern abolition societies. This question had become so alarming that the Governor thought it was time to bring the matter to a head.[20] The interest of the master and the slave required that the abolitionist be put down. This the Governor thought could not be done without the aid of the legislatures of the northern states. He therefore called upon them to pass such laws as would put a stop to the distribution of the papers. The legislature responded by drawing up a long preamble and a set of seven resolutions. In the preamble the committee said that the state of North Carolina had a right to regulate slavery in any way it saw fit; to continue or to abolish, to modify or to mitigate it in any form or extent, without reference to any earthly authority, and was solely responsible to its own conscience and the judgment of the Governor of the Universe. The claim upon the sister states, it thought, was just as clear as though they were foreign states.[21] The preamble stressed the phase of International Law. The resolutions said that North Carolina was ready to make a common cause with other slaveholding states in order to regulate slavery within its border. The kindest feeling was held toward the citizens of the northern states who had expressed abhorrence of the activities of the abolition societies. The northern states were respectfully requested to pass such penal laws as would prevent the circulation of publications which might incite the slaves to insurrection.[22] North Carolina depended upon the slaveholding states to unite in the protection of their own interest and present a united front.

Alabama thought just as North Carolina did that the abolitionist might be controlled by laws passed in the North. The legislature sent a memorial to the northern states, maintaining that slavery was a local and sectional matter, and meddling by

---

[19]*Niles Register*, XLIX, 245. The correspondent said it was learned that these resolutions were passed by unanimous consent.

[20] *Niles Register*, LXIX, 228. He said, upon this question there is no diversity of interest, and can be no difference of opinion. He told his legislature that the entire South would unite upon whatever task they undertook.

[21] *Laws of North Carolina*, November, 1835, 119. First of the resolutions.

[22] *Niles Register*, XLIX, 309.

persons who lived in the northern states could not be permitted. The legislature argued that if slavery was a wrong thing, then it was for Alabama herself to set it right.[23] Alabama wished help in the suppression of the disturbers, but this help had to be given in the way that Alabama demanded. The state of Mississippi also asked for aid from the northern states. It asked that the northern states pass such laws as would protect the state from the disturbance of the abolition papers.[24] These resolutions were to be sent to all the states.

The state of Kentucky passed a set of resolutions, as the other states mentioned above had done. It did not, however, expect any help from the northern states. The committee to which had been referred that part of the governor's message dealing with abolition said it did not plan to discuss the question of the right to hold slaves in Kentucky and held itself responsible only to the Ruler of the Universe. If the states were bound by no common bonds, they would still be bound by the principles of International Law which would prevent the citizens of the North from committing acts of which some of them had been guilty. The committee was convinced by many actions that there could be passed no laws in the North. This report was made in order that the southern states might know that Kentucky stood with them.[25] The resolutions followed very closely the preamble and asserted that the commonwealth of Kentucky had the power to regulate slavery within its boundary, and any attempt of the Federal Government to interfere with it in any manner would be at war with the solemn sanctions of that instrument which bound the states together. The southern states where slavery existed were assured that Kentucky supported them at all hazards.[26]

The Kentucky resolutions differed from the others in its purpose, but agreed with them in the authority to call upon the northern states if Kentucky thought that policy necessary. It would have depended upon the principles of International Law. This idea seemed to underlie the principles of all of the resolutions. The other southern states did not pass memorials to the northern states. However, this method was looked upon as one which

[23] *Senate Documents*, 124, 11, 24 Congress, 1st Session.
[24] *Laws of Mississippi*, 1836, 101. The preamble is very short and only one resolution dealing with slavery. The other two direct the governor to send the resolution to the states.
[25] *Laws of Kentucky*, 1835, 683; Resolutions.
[26] *Senate Document* 249, 111, 24 Congress, 1st Session.

would bring the abolition societies under control. There were some who felt that there could be no hope of obtaining the passage of laws in that section. Sargent said that at the time four-fifths of the people in the free states were opposed to slavery, although they did not think it was a good policy to meddle with it.[27] This shows that, in spite of the fact that the southern states had called for laws, some citizens did not expect them to be enacted. The southern states of Tennessee and Louisiana, did not request such laws.[28] If the North had passed these laws, there would have been no place where abolitionist papers could have been printed.

The North was also opposed to the abolitionists, as shown by the many meetings held in the North during the late summer of 1835. Would it pass laws to restrain the abolitionist? One of the first of the northern states to face this problem was Ohio. The legislature of that state met on December 7, 1835. Governor Lucas in his message to the legislature called attention to the condition of slavery in the southern states and related the fact that they had called for help. He thought as citizens of a common country this condition could not be viewed with indifference. The conduct of misguided individuals residing in the free states was sincerely denounced. The people of Ohio had stamped their conduct with the seal of disapprobation, and he thought they would continue to do so.[29] The method by which this would be done was moral force and public opinion, for no legislative act like that suggested by some of the southern states could be passed. This was prohibited by the constitution of Ohio and was not even a subject for discussion.[30] The governor called attention to another matter, the idea expressed by some of the southern states that certain abolition leaders could be transported from the state where they resided to the southern states. The governor reminded his legislature that such a request could not be granted.[31] The only remedy which the governor had to offer the legislatures of the

[27] Sargent, *Public Men and Events*, 294.

[28] *Resolves of Maine*, 1834-36, 119. Missouri and Maryland did not ask for law, at least no request was found.

[29] Governor's Message, *Ohio Senate Journal*, 1835-36, extract dealing with slavery. *Niles Register*, XLIX, 291.

[30] *Constitution of Ohio*, Article VIII, Sec. 6. The printing press shall be open and free to every citizen who wishes to examine it. Every citizen has an indisputable right to speak as he thinks proper, being liable for that privilege. *Statutes of Ohio*, XXII, 25.

[31] *Ibid.*, Sec. 17. That no person shall be liable to transportation out of this state for any offence committed within the state.

South was the observance of the Constitution, a procedure which he thought would solve the problem confronting the South.

The governor presented to the legislature the resolutions from the several states with the messages of their governors.[32]   The legislature referred to a committee these resolutions and also as much of the governor's message as dealt with antislavery papers.

At a large mass meeting held in Cincinnati the people had passed a set of proposals after the fashion of the southern resolutions.[33]   The preamble said it was a breach of political contract and a violation of faith to disturb the internal condition of the slaveholding states—both impolitic and ruinous to the southern states.   The South, because of its climate and position, had property in slaves; this property was guaranteed by the Constitution. The resolution expressed the belief that something should be done by those persons who lived in the northern states.[34]   This was a sentiment different from that coming from the governor, but it was also referred to the committee that in considering the question the different expressions in the state might be made known.

The committee labored with these messages and resolutions for some time.   Finally it made a report to the legislature.   It said that the state of Ohio had no power to legislate on the subject of slavery because of the Northwest Ordinance, because of the feelings of the people, and because of the constitution of the state.[35]   The committee agreed that these were troublesome problems but thought it was better to suffer the errors of judgment than to commit a greater evil.   The rule of International Law under which these demands were made scarcely applied.   The matter was taken up in the Ohio Legislature, but no law was passed.   A copy of these resolutions was to be sent by the governor of Ohio to the governors of the various states.[36]

The legislature of New York had to face the question of the resolutions when it met.   What New York did was of the greatest importance, for most of the papers were printed there.   Governor Marcy realized the importance attached to the action of New York

[32] *Ohio Senate Journal*, 1835-1836, 330.   December 30, 1835, South Carolina; January 28, 1836, North Carolina; Georgia, February 10; Alabama, March 2, 1836; Virginia, Kentucky, March 14.   The dates that resolutions were sent to the legislature by the governor.
[33] *Ohio Senate Journal*, 1835-1836, 564.
[34] *Ibid.*, 565.
[35] *Ohio Senate Journal*, 990.
[36] *Ibid.*, 991.

and his own message. He wrote to Van Buren and said that part of his own message to the legislature which had to deal with abolition was a very delicate matter. He thought that Van Buren and Butler, the Attorney-General, were in a position to give advice.[37] Marcy thought in relation to state matters it would be better to maintain silence, but such a method would not satisfy the responsible men of the South. He closed by expressing the hope he would hear from one of them on such an important subject; and he really had hopes of hearing from both of them. Marcy wrote Van Buren again December 3, and agreed with Van Buren that it was possible to speak upon the subject of slavery. He still expressed fear that part of his message might fall short of what the South expected, and if so it would hurt more than silence.[38] In spite of his own conviction, Marcy was willing to carry out the wishes of Van Buren in preference to his own views.

Marcy, in his annual message to the legislature, speaking upon this question, said he could not doubt that the legislature possessed the power to pass such laws as would prevent the citizens of the state of New York from availing themselves of the protection of its laws while they were fomenting insurrection in a sister state.[39] He would punish the abolitionists not only if they were engaged in producing in any way literature which might be distributed either then or later. Marcy had spoken the language of the South, for he, like the governors of the southern states, had spoken of the sovereignty of the state, which was after all the very basis of the "States' Rights" doctrine.

C. Rives said he was indebted to Van Buren for Marcy's message and that he thought it an admirable address and by far the most complete attack on abolition that the controversy had brought forth. It was hoped this would do much good in the North, coming from a northern man.[40] It had already done much good in the South by counteracting the nullifiers. It can be seen what part this policy played in determining the message of the governor and how it was used to mould sentiment in favor of the party in power.

The legislature referred as much of the governor's message as dealt with abolition to a committee. This committee presented a

[37] Van Buren MSS., Vol. 22. Letter dated Albany, November 22, 1832.
[38] Van Buren MSS., Vol. 22. Library of Congress.
[39] *New York American*, January 21, 1831.
[40] Van Buren MSS., XXII, letter to Van Buren, January 29, 1836.

set of resolutions to the legislature which was passed by the senate on May 19, 1836. The legislature restated the sentiment expressed in the governor's message, that every state had a right to regulate the relation of master and servant within its own limits. It was the concern of the legislature of each state as to whether slavery should be abolished or not, the welfare of the state being the determining factor.[41] The people of the state of New York, by responding to those views, had manifested their intention to keep from a discussion of the subject of domestic slavery. The resolutions closed with the argument that there was no necessity of any laws.[42] In spite of the message of the governor that the legislature had the power to pass a law against the abolitionists, none was passed.

The legislature of Massachusetts was confronted with the same question when it met in September, 1835, in a special session, and in January, 1836, in the regular session. Lieutenant-Governor Samuel Armstrong called attention to the disturbances in the country in his address. He said to allay this excitement by any suitable means was the duty of patriotic men, but he did not call for any special mode of procedure.[43] In January the state had a new governor, Edward Everett. In his message he called attention to the excitement kindled on the subject of the incendiary papers in different parts of the country; this excitement could not be too strongly deplored nor too severely censured. Slavery existed in some of the states prior to the Constitution and they came into the Union notwithstanding its existence, which was, he thought, a sanction of slavery. The governor asked that a forbearance with regard to this subject be maintained in the non-slaveholding states in order to strengthen the hands of slaveholding states.[44] The liberals in the South were willing and were actually working toward abolition, but this action on the part of the abolition societies had brought this work to a close. The governor would leave the whole matter to the Constitution of the United States.

The legislature took up the matter and referred as much of

[41] Laws of New York, 59th Session, 1836, 811, concurrent resolutions.
[42] Laws of New York, 59th Session, 1836, 812. Approved by the Assembly May 23, 1836.
[43] Niles Register, XLIX, 21. This was a special session for the revision of the statutes. Armstrong became acting governor March 3, 1835. His message in Laws of the Commonwealth of Massachusetts, 215.
[44] Laws of the Commonwealth of Massachusetts, 297-98. The message of Governor Everett, January 15, 1836.

the governor's message as dealt with slavery and all other documents which were transmitted by the governor on the subject to a special committee to investigate the matter. The committee was appointed January 16, the next day after the governor's message was given, and began work. Other abolition documents were referred to it as they came from the states.[45]

The Massachusetts Anti-Slavery Society became active in order, as the members thought, to prevent a law from being passed in favor of the southern states. The society justified its unusual action of seeking an interview with the legislative committee. They admitted that an interview would have been unnecessary in early times, but now freedom might not be maintained by the legislature of Massachusetts.[46] They were given their hearing; but it is difficult to tell whether it did any good, for there is every reason to think that no law such as the southern states asked for could have been passed in Massachusetts because the governor had not called for such a law and the state of Massachusetts had abolished slavery in 1783 by a court decision. The committee could only report that there was no necessity for a law, that there were enough laws; yet it admonished the citizens to refrain from meddling with the affairs of the South.[47] In spite of all efforts, the state of Massachusetts passed no law.

Governor Dunlap of Maine did not mention the slave question in his annual message but called attention to the slave question in a special message. He sent a very short message January 16, calling attention to the resolution from South Carolina.[48] He followed this method in the presentation of all the resolutions from the other southern states. He did not make a plea for them; he simply submitted them without comment and left it to the legislature to decide how it would handle the matter. The legislature had worked out its policy before the resolutions were presented to it. This was done when the South Carolina resolutions were presented by the governor. The legislature of Maine, unlike the legis-

[45] *Massachusetts Report on Slavery and Incendiary Literature*, 58.

[46] *Interview of Massachusetts Anti-Slavery Society with the Committee of Massachusetts Legislature, Boston, February*, 1836, 1.

[47] *Report of Massachusetts Legislative Committee on Slavery Publications*, 60.

[48] Resolves of 16th Legislature of Maine, 1835-36, 119. Special messages sent to the legislature on the following dates: South Carolina, January 16, 1835; North Carolina, January 27, 1836; Georgia, January 28; Alabama, February 17; Virginia, March 4; Kentucky, March 22; Mississippi, April 1.

latures of other northern states, passed a set of resolutions for the benefit of the southern states, but, like them, could not close the freedom of speech.[49] The select joint committee made its report on March 1. The report, like many of the reports from other northern states, said that slavery was a state matter and belonged to those states where it was approved by the individual state laws. Slavery was a question in which Maine had no interest; the citizens of Maine had no right to interfere with the internal regulations of other states. These were the sentiments of a large mass of persons, the committee thought.[50] It was easy to arrive at this conclusion because many meetings held in various parts of the state in the previous summer held the same view.

The legislature took this report and passed a set of resolutions along the same line. The resolutions said the government of the United States was a government of enumerated, limited powers; but power in regard to slavery was not one of the enumerated powers of that government and slavery was left to the people where it existed. The states also were considered separately in their relations with each other. The legislature of Maine did not see the necessity of passing any laws to regulate slavery, since the people in the public meetings had put a stop to all discussion; and no papers were printed in the state.[51] With all of its apparent friendliness to the southern states, Maine had neither passed any law such as had been demanded nor had declared itself against the use of the mail, the question which had prompted the southern states to send the resolutions. The legislature of Maine, however, had given the resolutions of the various states consideration and had worked out a policy of disposing of the request of the southern states. Whenever a request was sent to Maine by one of the southern states asking that laws be passed against the abolition societies, a set of these resolutions which had been passed by the legislature of Maine was sent to the state making the request. This was a simple method of handling the matter. It was mandatory upon the governor of the state to forward these resolutions to all complaining states. Copies were also sent to the senators and the representatives in Congress from Maine. We find Senator

[49] *Resolves of 16th Legislature of Maine*, 1834-36, 49.
[50] *Ibid.*, 47; ch. 54. Select Committee Charles Jarvis, Levi Johnson, Frederick Greene, Rufus McEnter, Eliakim Scammon, Obed Wilson, Sewell Lake, Stephen C. Foster, Alfred Richardson, Nathan C. Flecter, Charles Gordon.
[51] Resolves of 16th Legislature of Maine, 1834-36, 49 ch. 55.

Ruggles introducing them in the Senate on April 8, 1836.[52] These Maine resolutions were spread far and wide.

The Vermont legislature passed a set of resolutions in answer to the request sent from the South. The resolutions differed from those of Maine; while those from Maine argued the nature of the government and attempted to explain why no law could be passed, those from Vermont said that neither the Congress of the United States nor the states of the South had any constitutional right to abridge the free expression or the transmission of them through the public mail.[53] The other northern states had handled these resolutions in a very evasive way; Vermont met the question directly. Resolutions were sent to all of the northern states asking that the abolitionist be punished and that the South be helped in the solution of her problem. The southern states had asked for legislation in the handling of a very delicate matter, and the northern states had not responded, most of them finding some way to evade the question.

The South was not satisfied with calling upon the northern states for laws but made an effort to strengthen her own laws. The northern states felt this was a southern question and should be left to the South to handle.[54] The southern papers thought that the North disturbed the public peace. Some of the southern papers agreed that the power to control the matter was in the police power of the state. The editor of the *Richmond Enquirer* wrote to Postmaster-General Kendall and stated if he could not apply a remedy, the South would have to apply one by prosecuting the postmaster for the violation of a state law.[55] On August 7, just three days later, this same paper criticized the action of the citizens of Charleston, but said the South was formulating certain measures for handling the situation.[56] It is evident that the South was determined to deal with the matter in its own way whether the North acted or not.

In 1835, Maryland made an effort to bring this question under the control of the state law. It was a crime in that state for any one knowingly to circulate or to assist in the circulation of any paper or pictorial representation, written or printed, of an

[52] *Congressional Globe*, 24th Congress, 1st Session, 1835-36, III, 293.
[53] *Laws of Vermont*, 1836, October Session, 44. *The Liberator*, December, 1836.
[54] *New York American*, September 18, 1835.
[55] Editorial, August 4, 1835.
[56] *Richmond Enquirer*, August 7, 1835.

inflammatory nature for the purpose of inciting people of color in that state to insurrection.[57] The punishment consisted of a term in the penitentiary of not less than ten nor more than twenty years, this penalty to be inflicted regardless of the purpose. Maryland went still further and made it a crime for any citizen of the state to distribute this objectionable literature not only in the state of Maryland but also in any state or territory of the United States. The same penalty was provided as was imposed on a person guilty of the same offense in the state of Maryland.[58] This last section of the law of Maryland could not be enforced; Maryland could not make a law against an act which, though a crime in the state, was not a crime beyond its borders. Maryland, therefore, could not reach the individual who committed such an act, since the act was not committed in that state.

Virginia took up this question in 1835, and the legislature of that state passed a law to prevent the distribution of these papers. The law said anyone in that state denying the right of the master to hold property in slaves was considered to have committed a crime whether the act was done in writing or by word of mouth. The penalty was severe for those persons known as abolitionists, for it was primarily against them that the law was directed. When the violation was committed in person by word of mouth, the fine was not less than fifty dollars nor more than two hundred dollars and confinement in prison for a term of not less than six months and not more than three years.[59] The penalty was different and more drastic for any who was caught circulating incendiary literature in the state of Virginia. He was guilty of a felony, and the penalty was a term in the penitentiary for a period of not less than two nor more than five years.[60] This law made it difficult for the abolition papers to circulate in that state. It did not apply to the Negro, for the state had a different law for him. He was to receive not more than thirty-nine lashes and to be transported and sold beyond the confines of the state under order of the governor. Virginia planned, therefore, not only to punish the Negro, but

[57] *Laws of Maryland,* 1835, ch. 325, sec. 1 and pamphlet. Any newspaper, handbill or other paper printed or written of an inflammatory character, having a tendency to create discontent, and stir up to insurrection, any of the people of color of this State and that every person that shall be duly convicted of this offence, shall be guilty of a felony.

[58] *Laws of Maryland,* 1835, ch. 325, sec. I and pamphlet.

[59] *Laws of Virginia,* 1835-36, 44, Act of March 23, 1836.

[60] *Laws of Virginia,* 1835-36, 44, sec. II of that act.

also to remove him from the state, so that he might not cause unrest among the slaves.

The state had made provision for the free Negroes and slaves who were detected in the distribution of this literature, and thus turned to the postmasters. The postmasters were to give notice to the justice of the peace when such papers came to his office. The justice of the peace was to inquire into the case and have the papers or books burned in his presence. If, after the papers were burned, it appeared that the person subscribing for the paper knew its character or received it with the intention of circulating it he was to be placed in the county jail and be dealt with according to the laws of the state.[61] The postmaster who did not carry out the provision of this law was to be fined. The last section of this comprehensive law invested any white person with the authority to arrest any person detected violating the first two provisions of the act. There was little hope of the circulation of this literature in Virginia.

Governor Swain of North Carolina in his annual message called attention to the abolition papers. He did not call for a new law, but depended upon the law of 1830.[62] This law was very comprehensive and there was little chance for the papers to circulate in that state. There were no laws passed concerning the Negro, for the legislature was satisfied with those in existence. The state of South Carolina made an effort to strengthen its laws so there would be no opportunity for these papers to reach the slaves. It already had laws regulating the circulation of incendiary literature; it had passed a regulation to keep slaves who visited the North from returning to the South. In 1835, the legislature of South Carolina passed a law prohibiting the citizens or any other person from bringing into that state slaves who had been north of the Potomac River, to the West Indies, Mexico, or the city of Washington. The penalty for the violation of this act was the payment of one thousand dollars and the forfeiture of each slave.[63] South Carolina was determined to control antislavery literature and to check the action of those who might bring disturbance to her slave population.

The state of Alabama had a law as early as 1832, punish-

---

[61] *Ibid.*, 44, sec. III.

[62] *Niles Register*, XLIX, 228.

[63] *Ibid.*, 472. *Laws of South Carolina*, 1835. This law, that of 1820, and the Seamans act had for their object the control of all slaves and incendiary publications within the borders of the state.

ing by death any person who was detected in the distribution of antislavery papers, tending to produce a conspiracy or insurrection or rebellion.[64] In order to strengthen the laws which it already had, the state passed another law which indicated that any person convicted of knowingly circulating these forbidden papers should be punished by a term in the penitentiary for not less than ten years. The penalty was just as severe, regardless of whether the person distributed the papers or had them for that purpose.[65] The law specified that whether the printing, writing, or engraving was on paper, cloth, wood, metal, or stone the law would encompass it.[66] The penalty in the latter law was not as severe as that in the former, but it was more specific and no doubt more rigidly enforced.

The state of Georgia did not make a new law to regulate this new problem but depended upon its old laws. The law in Georgia was aimed at the free Negroes and slaves who went out of the state and returned. They might be permitted to return if they had been only in adjoining states.[67] They could not return to Georgia if they had been in a western or northern state, however, without incurring a penalty, which was a fine of one hundred dollars. Should it develop that the person convicted could not pay, he was to be bound out until it was paid, and thirty days after the fine was paid if he had not left the state he would be convicted again.[68] Tennessee handled this question by passing a law similar to those of the other states. The penalty was for a period of not less than ten nor more than twenty years in the state penitentiary at hard labor. This went further than some of the other state laws and gave the same penalty named above for words, gestures and even sermons in the presence of slaves.[69] This law applied to the circulation of these papers in the free states and in the slave states. The law was comprehensive and reached every phase of the question.

Louisiana, Mississippi, and Kentucky passed no laws which might be remotely connected with the papers. These states had passed very severe laws in 1831 in the excitement of Nat Turner's insurrection and felt that they were sufficient for this situation.

[64] *Digest of the Laws of Alabama*, 1833, 110, John C. Aikin.
[65] *Digest of the Laws*, the C. C. Clay ed., 1843, 412.
[66] *Ibid.*, 266, sec. 2.
[67] *Laws of Georgia*, 1835, 266.
[68] *Ibid.*, 266, sec. 2.
[69] *Public Acts of Tennessee*, 1835-36, 145.

Missouri, even though a western state, was faced with this abolition question. There was nothing in the governor's message to the General Assembly in relation to this important matter.[70] Senator William K. Vanarsdall of the Eleventh District, which is located along the Mississippi River, introduced November 26, 1836, a bill to prohibit the publication, circulation, or promulgation of abolition doctrine. This was brought up November 29, and made the special order of the day for December 15.[71] The bill passed through both houses and became a law in February, 1837. The law was not as elaborate as the laws of some of the southern states. The law said that if any person should circulate by writing, speaking, or printing any facts or arguments, reasoning or opinions tending directly to excite any slave or slaves, or other persons of color in the state to insurrection, the same upon conviction was to be fined a sum not exceeding $2,000 and imprisoned in the state penitentiary for a period not exceeding two years.[72] The second offense was much more severe, for the penalty was twenty years; and the third offense brought imprisonment for life. Missouri was a slaveholding state, and any interference with the system would influence her economically. Most of the slaves lived along the Mississippi and the Missouri Rivers and Senator Vanarsdall came from that section of the state. There had also been trouble at Marion College in Marion County over the question of abolition. On May 21, 1836, at a public meeting at Palmyra a certain Muldron began to read an abolition paper, and in the confusion which followed Dr. Bosley was injured.[73] This probably had something to do with the action of the Senator from the Eleventh District.

Some of the states, in spite of the efforts to control the situation, believed that the proper way to deal with this matter was to call upon Congress for laws. North Carolina in the same document which it sent to the northern states called upon Congress for passage of such laws as were necessary to prevent the circulation of inflammatory publications through the post office.[74] Georgia said

[70] *The Messages and Proclamations of the Governors of the State of Missouri*, Volume I, 307. *First Biennial Message*, 44. The Eleventh District comprised the counties of Audrain, Pike and Lincoln.

[71] *Senate Journal of the General Assembly of Missouri*, 1836-1837, 57. It came up several times during the session.

[72] *Laws of Missouri*, 1836-37, 3.

[73] *Missouri Argus*, June 3, 1836.

[74] *Niles Register*, XLIX, 309.

in the report of a joint committee of the legislature, to which had been referred that part of the governor's message dealing with slavery, that it devolved upon Congress in the ensuing session to modify the laws regulating the post office. This was asked for by the South in order to prevent civil war and servile strife, the resolution said.[75]

All the states agreed that Congress had no right to interfere with slavery in the slave states.[76] Thus were directed the efforts of the states to control the distribuion of antislavery papers by state action.

[75] *Ibid.*, 245. Report of joint committee of the legislature on Federal relations.
[76] Governor McDuffie on the Slavery question, *America Historical Leaflet*, Number 10, 12.

CHAPTER V

THE CONTROVERSY IN CONGRESS

In spite of the efforts made by both the local communities and
the states to control the distribution of anti-slavery literature, it
was evident that the control of the papers would be a question
which would have to be dealt with in the first session of the 24th
Congress. The Postmaster-General in his annual report to
the President on the condition of the post office spoke of the confusion caused by the abolition papers and of the method with
which this matter had been handled. He called this a new problem which had arisen in the distribution of the mail. A new, rich
organization had developed, he said, in the North.[1] It is not surprising that the Postmaster-General was deceived as to the wealth
of this antislavery organization, for on one occasion the abolition
society had been able to call for thirty thousand dollars and had
secured it.[2] Then, too, the papers were being sent to the South
gratuitously. In his report the Postmaster-General based his entire argument upon the right of the states. It was the duty of the
National Government, he thought, to prevent the circulation of
these papers, certainly where it was prohibited by law. Their circulation would give the North an undue advantage, for it allowed
the discussion of a subject there which was denied the southern
states. Kendall, in his report, restated the instructions which he
had given to the postmasters at Charleston and at New York and
showed how helpless he had been in the crisis. The Postmaster-
General left the matter to Congress to work out as it saw fit.[3] It
was clear that the Postmaster-General, as he said in his letter to
Andrew Jackson, was willing to follow a vacillating policy which
would not offend the South.[4] He asked that Congress give this
question careful consideration, but laws were not demanded.[5]
Kendall was satisfied to handle the matter as he had done from

[1] Globe, Appendix, 24th Congress, 1st Session, 1835-36, III, 8.
[2] L. G. Tyler, *Life & Times of the Tylers*, I, 576.
[3] *Niles Register*, XLIX, 277.
[4] J. S. Bassett, *Correspondence of Andrew Jackson*, V, 359.
[5] *Niles Register*, XLIX, 278.

the beginning of the controversy, since it made for peace in the South. It is evident now that any law which might have been passed that did not exclude the papers from the South would have been objectionable to Kendall, as he was a protagonist of the "States' Rights" principle, interested in protecting his own adopted views.

In his seventh annual message Jackson took up this question to which the Postmaster-general had called his attention. He had become officially acquainted with the problem as early as August, when Kendall wrote him, reporting the prevailing excitement in the southern section of the country.[6] The President took the position that the action which the Postmaster-General had taken was correct and would serve until Congress met. Congress had now met, and it was only natural that the subject would be treated in his annual message. The President asked that a law be passed which would make it a crime to circulate through the mail incendiary publications with the purpose of inciting slaves to insurrection.[7] Peace could not be brought about, he urged, unless Congress passed some law to suppress these papers. Peace and happiness depended upon the maintenance of those compromises upon which the Union was founded. Jackson accused the abolition societies of attempting to stir up the slaves to insurrection and bring on a servile war.[8] The American Anti-Slavery Society of New York differed sharply from this indictment and insisted that the President had not even given it a chance for defense.[9] The letter declared that what had been done by this society was no secret. How could the abolitionists stir up the slaves to insurrection when no literature was addressed to them? Furthermore, were the slaves accustomed to receiving periodicals of any kind, whether incendiary or not, by mail?[10] The society denied vigorously that any of these papers were sent to slaves. If any of these were sent to free Negroes, there was no way for the societies to know.[11] The society could not find any evidence that their papers had been sent to Negroes, and if any were sent there was nothing in them that would excite the slaves to insurrection. It was argued that if any

[6] J. S. Bassett, *Correspondence of Andrew Jackson*, V, 360.
[7] J. D. Richardson, *Messages and Papers of the President*, IV, 1394.
[8] *Ibid.*, III, 175.
[9] W. Jay, *Miscellaneous Writings on Slavery*, 366.
[10] W. Jay, *Miscellaneous Writings on Slavery*, 366. The letter took up the contest thoroughly.
[11] Massachusetts Anti-Slavery Society, *Annual Report*, 1836, 17.

of the papers were sent to slaves, they would have been of little value, for most of the slaves could not read them. The President was invited to consult the southern papers and to get the names of the persons to whom material was sent. He would discover, the society contended, that those who were receiving this literature were not the slaves, but the public officers, clergymen, and other influential citizens.[12] This letter was of the greatest significance, for if the papers were not addressed to the slaves, what difference would it have made if they were sent to the South? The citizens to whom they were sent might have placed them in the waste basket or destroyed them and forgotten all about them. This would have solved the problem, since none of the papers could reach the slaves, and hence could do no harm. It seems that the leaders in the South wished to impress upon the leaders in the North that the question of slavery was not their affair and that it belonged exclusively to the South.

The President's message brought the matter directly before both branches of Congress. In the House the section dealing with the transmission of abolition papers through the mail was referred to the Committee on Post Offices and Post Roads.[13] In spite of the importance which the President attached to the matter, it got little consideration in the House, and therefore it attracted little attention in the country at large.[14] After the resolution was passed, nothing more was heard in the House from the committee to which this matter was referred until February 4, 1836, when Wise, of Virginia, asked its chairman if at this time a report could be made from the Committee on Post Offices and Post Roads.[15] The chairman replied that he did not know when such a report would be made. Here the matter rested until after Calhoun had made his report on incendiary papers in the Senate. The report of the Senate's special Committee agreed with the President that a law should be passed to regulate incendiary publications.[16] The bill reported contained nine sections. It pro-

[12] W. Jay, *Miscellaneous Writings on Slavery*, 368.
[13] *Globe*, 24th Congress, 1st Session, III, 26. The President's message was submitted to the committee of the House by a set of resolutions. The ninth resolution disposed of incendiary papers as referred to in the Postmaster-General's report and the President's message.
[14] *Ibid.*, 21. The members of the Committee on Post Offices and Post Roads were Connor of North Carolina, Briggs of Massachusetts, Laport of Pennsylvania, Hall of Vermont, Mann of New York, Cleveland of Georgia, French of Kentucky, Shields of Tennessee, and Hopkins of Virginia.
[15] *Ibid.*, 152.
[16] R. K. Cralle, *Calhoun Works*, IV, 510.

vided that it should not be lawful for any postmaster or deputy postmaster knowingly to receive and put into the mail any pamphlet, newspaper, handbill, or other printed, written, or pictorial representation touching the subject of slavery, directed to any person or post office, where by law thereof, their circulation was prohibited, or to deliver such papers to any person whatsoever, except such persons as might be authorized by proper authority of such states. The second section made it the duty of the Postmaster-General both to dismiss the deputy, or postmaster, and to fine him for violation of the first section of the law. The third section made it the duty of the postmasters to coöperate and to see that "incendiary literature" should not be circulated. Section four made it the duty of the Postmaster-General to furnish to the deputy postmasters copies of the laws of the state which prohibited the circulation of incendiary literature. The fifth section provided that the deputy postmaster should give notice to the Postmaster-General where pamphlets had been deposited. They might be withdrawn within a month by the persons depositing them, but if not withdrawn by the end of that time they were to be burned or otherwise destroyed.[17]

On February 19, Ingersoll, of Pennsylvania, moved that there should be printed for the House ten thousand extra copies of this report from the Senate's special committee.[18] The House, however, objected because it desired to evade the controversy. Ingersoll, not satisfied with the decision, made a motion to suspend the rules; it failed to pass. The matter was tabled until March 25, when it came before Congress in another way. Hall, of Vermont, a member of the Committee on Post Offices and Post Roads, called attention to that part of the President's message dealing with incendiary papers which had been referred to the committee of which he was a member and upon which the committee had up to this time not reported.[19] He asked to be allowed to do an unusual thing, to submit a minority report before the majority had reported. Hall gave as a reason his desire to make a report in order to set forth the views of those who differed from the Postmaster-General, the President, and Senator Calhoun. This extraordinary report came as a surprise to the entire House.

[17] Gales and Seaton, *Register of Debate*, XII, 364. Made in the Senate on February 4, 1836.

[18] *Globe*, 24th Congress, 1st Session, III, 174.

[19] *Ibid.*

The difficulties which the committee had experienced were brought to light. The chairman of the committee said that this subject had occupied much of the time of the committee for weeks, even for months; they had been ready to report but had lacked a single vote.[20] The House, true to the policy which it had maintained from the beginning, voted March 25, 1835, not to receive Hall's report for it was out of order.[21]

On May 21, the matter came up before the House again. At this time Shields, of Tennessee, amended the report of the committee.[22] He argued that the government had nothing to do with slavery in any of the other states, neither did any state have the right to interfere with slavery in any of the other states. The National Government should regulate the mail under the commerce powers of the Constitution; it could not, by so doing, interfere with slavery.[23] Hall, of Vermont, differed from the amendment offered by Shields, and seized upon the opportunity to state the views which he could not give in his attempted report. He agreed with that part of the argument of Shields which said that Congress had no constitutional power to interfere with slavery but differed with the part dealing with the power of Congress to act as a *censor of the press*. He thought that the postmaster had a right to see that the postage was collected, but the moment that he examined the mail to inspect its contents he had violated the Constitution of the United States and had become a censor of the press. He maintained that the state had sufficient power to regulate the matter; and therefore, he would not agree that Congress should pass any law until the states had exhausted all their power.[24] This amendment was not passed, and this closed the contest in the House. There were several efforts made to have the matter handled by the House, but all failed. That body stuck to its set policy, namely, to handle this matter through the regular committee.

The peaceful method which was so evident in the House did not prevail in the Senate. John C. Calhoun, a nationalist during the War of 1812, had now moved along with his section

[20] *Globe*, 24th Congress, 1st Session, III, 174.
[21] *Niles Register*, I, 79.
[22] *Globe*, 24th Congress, 1st Session, III, 391.
[23] *Ibid.* This matter was referred to the committee on December 17, 1835. March 25, Hall submitted his minority report.
[24] *Globe*, 24th Congress, 1st Session, III, 391. This came up in the General Post Office Bill. The Post Office was undergoing reorganization.

to the "States' Rights" point of view.[25]   He came to Congress
with a fixed principle and a definite plan for the relief of his
section.   In the Senate on December 21, 1835, he moved that that
part of the President's message which dealt with the transmission of incendiary papers through the public mails be referred
to a select committee.[26]   This was an unusual procedure because
the Senate, like the House, had a Committee on Post Offices and
Post Roads to which this matter should have ordinarily gone.
Calhoun gave as one reason for his desire to change the policy of
the Senate, that it was a question of a complicated nature and
as such did not properly come within the duties of the Committee on Post Offices and Post Roads.   Another reason which he
gave for his action was that the personnel of the committee was
unsatisfactory, that it had only one member from that section
most concerned.   This was even more plausible than the first argument.[27]

Senator King, of Alabama, differed from Calhoun and saw
no need for reference to a special committee. He contended that
he was as much interested in that subject as any other man on
the floor of the Senate but felt to refer it to a special committee would give it too much prominence. He admitted that Congress did not have the matter entirely in its hands, but could
handle it because such matters came under postal regulations.
He accused Calhoun of being entirely too hasty in his actions,
and insisted further that if the regular committee refused to
act within a reasonable time after the matter had been referred
to it, then and not until then, should a special committee be summoned.[28]   This objection on the part of King was of importance,
for it came from one who lived in the same section as Calhoun
and was just as interested in its protection of the "States'
rights" principle.

The attack by King forced Calhoun to find another reason for
the departure from the regular procedure.   He claimed not to
have considered party lines at all, but only to have wished a commission which would have time to consider calmly and to examine

[25] H. Von Holst, *John C. Calhoun*, American Statesmen.
[26] *Globe*, 24th Congress, 1st Session, III, 36.
[27] T. H. Benton, *Abridgment of the Debates of Congress*, XII, 703. The
Senate Post Office and Post Roads Committee was composed of the following: Grundy of Tennessee (Chairman); Robinson, Illinois; Ewing, Ohio;
Knight, Rhode Island; and Davis, Massachusetts.
[28] *Globe*, 24th Congress, 1st Session, III, 36.

the question carefully. He felt that the regular committee would be occupied with the regular business which would come before it, but that a group devoting all of its time to this measure could report more quickly and with more thoroughness than one burdened with other tasks.[29] Grundy, the chairman of the committee on Post Offices and Post Roads, differed very sharply from Calhoun. He felt the subject was an important one and needed careful study, but opposed the motion for a special organization. He thought the subject could be better studied by those from a more or less disinterested section of the country. This would give the report more influence in the country. Grundy, like most of the men who preceded him, restated the well-known maxim that Congress had no power to deal with slavery. Grundy realized that if the matter were handled by the committee on Post Offices and Post Roads, it would fall to him. He, however, neither sought the favor nor dodged the responsibility.[30] Clayton of Delaware said that it was agreed that the subject involved Constitutional law and thought it should be sent to a special committee. He thought the report would be more satisfactory to the people if it came from a committee from the slaveholding section.[31] After much debate the vote was taken and Calhoun was able to have his way. On motion of Calhoun the committee was to consist of five members.[32]

That Calhoun had given this subject special consideration is evident, for as early as August 30, 1835, one month after the affair in Charleston, he had written to Duff Green, commenting upon the excitement caused by the fanatics of the North.[33] Calhoun in this same letter insisted that the South would present a united front even to the point of disunion. He hoped, however, that secession would not be necessary. Calhoun had worked out a plan and wanted the matter entrusted to him so that he might express the southern doctrine on the slave question. He knew that if a special committee were created, he would be made its chairman and would be able to direct its policies. This was a

[29] T. H. Benton, *Abridgment of the Debates of Congress*, XII, 703.

[30] *Globe*, 24th Congress, 1st Session, III, 36.

[31] *Ibid.*, 37. There were arguments pro and con, northern Senators generally opposing and the southern favoring a special committee.

[32] T. H. Benton, *Abridgment of Debates of Congress*, XII, 704. Twenty-three voted for the measure. There were thirty-five Senators present on the opening day. Several states had only one Senator.

[33] Correspondence of J. C. Calhoun, 1899, in the American Historical Society, *Annual Report*, II, 345.

long standing custom in the Senate, as it still is in deliberative bodies, that the person who asks for a special committee to investigate a matter in which he is interested is made chairman of the committee. The committee was composed of Calhoun, King of Georgia, Mangum of North Carolina, Davis of Massachusetts, and Linn of Missouri—a committee made up, with one exception, of persons from the slaveholding states.[34] Davis was the only person who was both a member of the Committee on Post Offices and Post Roads and of the special committee.[35] The political complexion of the committee was as follows: Calhoun claimed no party but was opposed to the administration; Mangum and Davis were members of the Whig party; Linn and King were Jackson Democrats; thus the committee was so composed that there was little chance for a party measure.[36]

The motives of Calhoun in taking upon himself the direction of this contest have been variously interpreted. Whether Calhoun was influenced by a desire to lay the foundation for a southern confederacy or merely used this method to influence feeling against Jackson, as Bowers thinks, can never be known.[37] The southern people looked upon slavery as a part of their social fabric and had begun to regard it as absolutely necessary to their institutions. Calhoun was simply expressing the public opinion of his section.[38] Calhoun said that the safety of the slaveholding communities required above all things that the Negroes should not know there was a plan on foot to give them their freedom; if they did they would try to set themselves free.[39] It was probably all of these motives which influenced the action of Calhoun.

There is another factor that gave Calhoun some concern at this time—the railroad. Charleston, Calhoun's adopted city, had lost a part of its commerce to New Orleans and that city had become the chief commercial city of the South.[40] This had been true because of its connection with the West by means of the Missis-

[34] *Globe*, 24th Congress, 1st Session, III, 37.

[35] Gale and Seaton, *Abridgment of Debates in Congress*, XII, 33. The importance of the personnel comes out when the report is made.

[36] These are the parties given by the *Appleton Cyclopedia of American Biography*. E. A. Linn and N. Sargeant, *The Life and Public Services of Dr. Lewis Linn*, 78.

[37] *Party Battles of the Jackson Period*, 444.

[38] C. H. Peck, *Jacksonian Epoch*, 273.

[39] G. Hunt, *John C. Calhoun*, 229.

[40] R. S. Cotterill, "Railroads and Western Trade," *Mississippi Valley Historical Review*, 1840-1851, III, 429.

sippi River. It was conceived by influential citizens of Charleston, South Carolina, that one way to restore Charleston to her former place was the connection of Charleston with the West. As early as 1835 Hayne and Calhoun had projected the Charleston and Cincinnati Railroad to run from Charleston through western North Carolina, Tennessee, and Kentucky to Cincinnati.[41] Carter, a citizen of Georgia, was anxious that the railroad should pass by way of northern Georgia. Calhoun, speaking in reference to the railroad, said that on the questions of the railroad and of slavery the South had to stand together even if it differed on every other question.[42] The legislature of South Carolina in December, 1835, passed a provision for the survey of a route for the proposed Charleston and Cincinnati Railroad.[43] The commission was composed of Robert Y. Hayne, Patrick Noble, Thomas Smith, Abraham Blanding, Charles Edmonston, and Thomas F. Jones. The act regulating the Charleston, Louisville, Cincinnati Railroad was amended in December, 1836, and allowed the road to be built by touching Kentucky only at Lexington.[44] There was much enthusiasm about this railroad in the West. For this section it meant the possibility of building a railroad toward the East.[45] Calhoun saw clearly that there would be a division in the state over this railroad, as Savannah, Georgia, wanted to be the terminus and disputed Charleston's right to it. Calhoun sought to weld together his people on a basis of the economic interests of their section. The South, regardless of party lines, had come to regard slavery as necessary to its welfare and did not wish it to be eradicated.[46] Calhoun no doubt felt that the South must unite on important issues and that the railroad was one of the most important issues for that section and a principal issue for Charleston, since the salvation of the city was at stake.

February 4, 1836, Calhoun reported from the special committee on incendiary papers.[47] He explained his proposed bill in a long report agreeing with that part of the President's message

[41] R. S. Cotterill, ''Southern Railroads and Western Trade,'' *Mississippi Valley Historical Review*, 1840-1851, III, 429.

[42] *Correspondence of J. C. Calhoun*, II, 344.

[43] *Laws of South Carolina*, 1835, 16.

[44] *Ibid.*, 42; U. B. Phillips, *History of Transportation in the Eastern Cotton Belt to 1860*, 179.

[45] *Southern Patriot*, March 9, 1836.

[46] W. E. Dodd, *Statesmen of the Old South*, 134.

[47] *Niles Register*, XLIX, 408.

which said that the abolition papers were dangerous to the welfare and peace of the South, but not agreeing with the remedy which the President thought was applicable. The committee insisted that Congress should pass no law to redress the grievance of the South, for any law which it might pass would be an abridgment of the freedom of speech and of the press which was left with the states exclusively. If Congress should have passed such a law the committee felt that it would have broken down all the barriers which the slaveholding states had erected for themselves.[48] It was left to the state to determine what should be classified as literature calculated to disturb their peace and quietness. This power was not among the enumerated powers, and the government was bound to respect whatever measures the states should adopt for their protection. The report went to great length into an exposition on slavery and the relation between the states. Calhoun had developed his doctrine that slavery was under the sole and exclusive control of the states where it existed and that these states should determine what means they would use to defend themselves.[49]

With this report a bill containing five sections for the regulation of those objectionable papers was reported. This bill made it unlawful for any deputy postmaster knowingly to place in the mail any pamphlet, memorial, or newspaper, touching upon the question of slavery, or to send it where such was prohibited by the laws of the state. Any postmaster violating this law was to be fined and dismissed from the service.[50] The Postmaster-General under the law must dismiss any postmaster who should violate this provision, and if he were convicted he was to be fined.[51] The postmasters and deputy postmasters were expected to coöperate as much as possible to prevent the circulation of incendiary literature. They could not be protected under the rules of the post office if they knowingly sent this material where it was prohibited by law. The Postmaster-General, under this law, had to furnish to every postmaster of every state where this type of mail was prohibited by statute a copy of the law. The proposed law further stated that Congress had no right to make any law to regulate the

[48] *Report of Special Committee on Abolition Papers*, 24th Congress, 1st Session; also Senate Bill, 122, Library of Congress Toner Collection.
[49] *Globe*, 24th Congress, 1st Session, III, 150; *Senate Journal*, 24th Congress, 1st Session, I, 138.
[50] T. H. Benton, *Abridgment of Debates in Congress*, XII, 720.
[51] *Ibid.*, XII, 720, sec. 2. The amount of the fine was left blank, both upper and lower amount.

post office, although the bill, had it passed, would have definitely regulated the mail and post offices.[52]

The reason for the committee's tardiness in reporting became evident when the bill was reported. Mangum of North Carolina, who agreed in every respect with the bill and the report, moved that 5,000 extra copies of both be printed.[53] At this point in the discussion King, of Georgia, said that in order that a misunderstanding might not go abroad in reference to his views he wished to state in the report that he did not assent entirely.[54] Davis said that he differed from the chairman and would have made a separate report but felt it would do no good, and thus did not follow the usual course. Linn of Missouri also said that he did not agree with it in all respects.[55] This was a peculiar type of procedure. The bill was rejected in whole or in part by a majority of the committee, yet it was reported. Calhoun agreed that the majority was not in favor of the report and the bill; some opposed the bill while others approved the report.[56] This explains why the committee was so long reporting. In spite of difficulty Calhoun had been able to have his way. Clay said that reports were simply argumentative papers and were not considered as adopted paragraph by paragraph when they were ordered printed. With this explanation and with the modification of the motion to print so as to include the report also, the motion passed.[57]

Calhoun was in a very difficult position, for he opposed the law recommended by the President, and as a leader of southern thought, he had to do something in the way of suggesting a plan to settle the controversy. The President had asked that Congress pass a law which would make the dispatching of abolition papers a crime punishable by a fine or imprisonment. Calhoun had insisted that the passage of a law, such as the President had asked for, was an attack on the principle of the freedom of the press and the rights of the states. He would solve this problem by allowing the papers to be sent wherever it was not contrary to the laws of the state. Calhoun held that Congress could not make laws which conflicted with the state laws, and if such were made,

[52] *Globe*, 24th Congress, 1st Session, III, 151.
[53] T. H. Benton, *Abridgment of Debates in Congress*, 721.
[54] T. H. Benton, *Thirty Years' View*, I, 581.
[55] *Globe*, 24th Congress, 1st Session, III, 150.
[56] *Globe*, 24th Congress, 1st Session, III, 150.
[57] T. H. Benton, *Abridgment of Debates in Congress*, XII, 721.

the National law must give way to the State.[58]   This is the reverse
of the view at that time held by some authorities, and now generally held.[59]   The distinction between the jurisdiction of the
state and the National Government was not so clearly determined
then as it is now. Calhoun believed that the state law was superior
to national law, especially when the conflict involved slavery. He
arrived at this conclusion from that clause of the Constitution
which empowers Congress to make all laws which shall be necessary and proper for carrying into execution the powers vested by
the Constitution in the Government of the United States. He considered the law-making power of the National Government as
delegated to it by the states.[60] From this point of view it is easy
to see why the state laws stood first with Calhoun.[61]   The principle was, he contended, that the Constitution was made by the
states and as sovereign bodies the states created a governmental
agent for their general welfare. The term United States was only
the name of the general governmental agent of the states; sovereignty was in the states only.

The report and the resolution were received by the Senate
and remained upon the calendar from February 4 to April 4, a
period of two months, before Calhoun called them up for consideration by the Senate.[62] When the bill was brought up Davis was
the first to attack it. He insisted that the bill was too broad in its
scope and that it applied to any subject touching the question of
slavery. It would prohibit the circulation of an essay on education or the Declaration of Independence and would make an in-
quisition out of a branch of the National Government. The postmaster in order not to violate this act would have to inspect all
the mail which might pass through his office.[63] This was a criticism of the bill by one who had been a member of the committee
and who was familiar with the bill from all angles. Calhoun
admitted that Davis had raised a very interesting point and one
difficult to answer.[64]

[58] *Niles Register*, XLIX, 409.
[59] T. M. Cooley, *Constitutional Limitations*, 416.
[60] Calhoun, *Works*, II, 269.
[61] H. Von Holst, *John C. Calhoun*, American Statesmen Series.
[62] *Globe*, 24th Congress, 1st Session, III, 279. Calhoun gave notice on
April 4 that he would call it up when the expunging resolution was finished.
April 6, Calhoun put the amount of the fines in his bill not less than $100
nor more than $1,000.
[63] *Ibid.*, 288.
[64] T. H. Benton, *Abridgment of Debates in Congress*, XII, 754.

Senator King, of Georgia, another member of the special committee, said that he intended to vote for the bill but could not support the principles of the report, for he felt that the report was inconsistent with the bill. King doubted if the National Government could last twelve months operating under the provisions of the law which Calhoun had proposed, because it would set up a permanent conflict between the national and state governments. The bill, he thought, supported the policy of the President's message, which called for Congress to pass a law to regulate the distribution of incendiary papers, while the report argued against the bill.[65] King attributed this inconsistency between the bill and the report to Calhoun's dislike for Jackson. He said that when Calhoun began to examine the subject he found the President's message correct and, knowing the public sentiment of the South, dared not report a bill. Therefore, he elected to report a bill such as the South demanded and then presented his own ideas in a report.[66] There was so much in the bill that conformed to the President's message one wonders why Calhoun did not come out wholeheartedly and support the message. This argument by King forced Calhoun to show the motive which had actuated him. The motives attributed to him were vigorously denied by the senator.[67] He insisted that in the late summer of 1835 he knew the slavery question would be important and would force itself upon Congress. He stated that he had studied the matter and had come to the conclusion that a law would be made to regulate these abolition papers. Calhoun was convinced that Congress had no power to make such a law and furthermore if such a law were made it would be useless, and so he intended to do all in his power to prevent it. He said he knew well how apt the weak and timid were, in a state of excitement and alarm, to seek temporary protection in any quarter regardless of consequences, and how ready the artful and designing ever were to seize on such occasions to extend and perpetuate their power. With these impressions he arrived at the beginning of the session. Calhoun said the President assumed for Congress direct power over the subject, and that on the broadest, most unqualified and dangerous principles. Calhoun says, "knowing the influence of his name by reason of his great patronage and the rigid discipline of his party with a large

[65] *Globe*, Appendix, 24th Congress, 286. King's speech is given in full.
[66] T. H. Benton, *Abridgment of Debates in Congress*, XII, 756.
[67] R. K. Cralle, *Works of John C. Calhoun*, II, 509.

portion of the country, who have scarcely any other standard of
constitution, politics, or morals, I saw the full extent of the danger of having these dangerous principles reduced to practice, and
I determined at once to use every effort to prevent it.''[68] Calhoun
hoped to control the situation by the creation of a special committee and thus prevent the passage of any law unless it conformed to his own idea. It was no doubt true that he had studied
the situation carefully. He wrote to Mrs. Ann C. Calhoun on
January 25, 1836, in reply to a letter in which she had suggested
that it would be better for the country to allow the South to
depart in peace than that the sections should go on as they were
then. The Senator agreed with her that this was a natural and
common conclusion for those who had not thought of the difficulties involved. He, too, agreed that the South and the North ought
not live together in such a condition as described, but thought the
South should do all it could to arrest this natural tendency and to
justify itself before God and man.[69] On February 7, three days
after he had made his report from the special committee about the
condition of slavery, he wrote to Christopher Van Deventer, who
had been chief clerk of the War Department during Calhoun's
administration. He said that Van Deventer gave a fearful picture
of the progress of the fanatics which was confirmed from every
section of the South. Calhoun feared that a direct issue between
the North and the South could not long be delayed; and if it came
it would destroy the political fabric, or if it did stop short of that
it would shake the country to its center. Calhoun said that he had
discussed some important points in his report and thought it was
well received on all sides.[70] Calhoun wrote J. H. Hammond February 18, two days after the latter had resigned from the House
on account of ill health, and said he saw nothing but the abolition
question and never had but one opinion on the subject. The fate
of the South as a people was tied up in the question; if she
yielded her people would be exterminated, but if she could successfully resist they would be the greatest and most flourishing
people of modern times.[71] When the session was almost closed,
Calhoun wrote to Amisted Burt, a Calhoun Democrat, who became
a member of the House from 1843 to 1853, that he was glad his

[68] R. K. Cralle, *Works of John C. Calhoun*, II, 509.
[69] American Historical Association, *Annual Report*, II, 291.
[70] *Ibid.*, 1899, II, 357.
[71] American Historical Association, *Annual Report*, II, 357.

constituents had approved of the action he had taken during the session. In this same letter, he said he was of the impression that much had been effected during the session and thought the South was better united, but must not relax. The abolitionists, he said, were numerous, zealous, and active and had a powerful press and abundant funds.[72] In all of these letters Calhoun showed that he had studied the question and had one objective, to unite the South on the one common issue.

In spite of all we know of his interest in the question and his argument to the contrary, he does not clear himself completely of the charge made by King that hostility to Jackson was the cause for the long report and the bill. He showed his hostility later on in his speech when he said he had made the report because the composition of the committee made it evident that a bill would be reported after the fashion of the President's message. He had elected to report the bill as the committee wanted and expressed his opinion in a report. Calhoun said he must tell the Senator from Georgia that he had too little regard for the opinion of General Jackson, and, were it not for his high station, he would add his character too, to allow his course to be influenced by Jackson either for or against the measure.[73] That Calhoun was hostile to the President no one can deny, but it is reasonable to suppose that Calhoun, as the spokesman of the South and the defender of his pet theory, the rights of the state, approached the problem from that angle.

Much of the time of the Senate was taken up with a discussion of antislavery petitions, and the discussion of the incendiary literature was sidetracked for a while. The distribution discussion was participated in by many Senators. Buchanan argued for the bill but on different grounds from those of King and Calhoun, who spoke from the "States' Rights" angle. He said Congress could make any law it desired to regulate the post office over which it had exclusive control. It was necessary that Congress pass a law which would make the circulation of incendiary papers a penal offense and thus relieve the states of the responsibility which they had assumed.[74] Under the bill, Congress would neither protect the postmasters who knowingly violated the law nor force any postmaster to distribute the abolition papers where they were prohibited by law. Buchanan stood for the passage of the bill on

[72] Ibid., 361.
[73] Works of Calhoun, II, 513.
[74] James Buchanan's Works, edited by J. B. Moore, II, 83.

exactly the same grounds the President recommended and not on those which Calhoun had advanced.[75] This is easily understood because Buchanan was strictly a party man and followed the Administration while Calhoun opposed it. Buchanan further contended that the bill would not violate the freedom of the press, for anyone could write what he pleased and put it in the post office; the post office, however, was not forced to circulate what was written.[76] The position which Buchanan took was sound when applied to the interpretation of the law in our own day, for now a number of things can be kept out of the mails. In former times it was not clearly defined just how far Congress could go in the exclusion of materials from the National Post Office. If these papers could be excluded, they were partly denied the right of circulation without which the right of publication is barren. Buchanan said he was willing to vote against the circulation if that would bring peace and harmony to the southern states and prevent an uprising in that section.[77] The duty of the Federal Government to the states in this matter was perfectly clear to Buchanan.

Grundy argued for the bill because the authority of Congress over the post office was complete and there was no way for the state authority and the national authority to conflict. The bill, he said, simply gave Congress power to do legally what the postmaster had done without law in the summer of 1835.[78] Later on in the course of discussion of this bill Grundy argued that this bill was not directed against the freedom of the press but simply said to the employees of the post office that their Government would not protect them if they violated the laws of the states.[79] The argument was very much like that of Buchanan.

Cuthbert of Georgia insisted that the law was for the purpose of preventing the postmasters from committing a criminal act. He contended that the postmaster must determine whether these papers were legal or not.[80] Many others, in the course of the long debate, argued for the bill, but most of them restated the arguments already made.

There were others who argued against the bill, the most noted of whom were Webster, Benton, and Clay. Webster attacked the

---

[75] *Globe*, Appendix, 24th Congress, 1st Session, III, 437.
[76] G. T. Curtis, *Life of James Buchanan*, I, 342.
[77] *James Buchanan's Works*, II, 85 cf.
[78] T. H. Benton, *Abridgment of Debates in Congress*, XII, 759.
[79] *Globe*, Appendix, 24th Congress, 1st Session, III, 549.
[80] *Ibid.*, 441.

bill from the point of view of its indefiniteness. The bill made it mandatory for the postmaster to know the laws of every state so that he might not send these papers where they were prohibited.[81] Webster contended that the bill was too comprehensive, for it applied to every paper, handbill, or pictorial representation if it touched the subject of slavery in any shape or form, either for or against the subject. This restriction might extend to any publication. Even the Constitution of the United States might be prohibited from the mail, and the person who was to decide this important question was the Deputy Postmaster or the clerk. He feared that Congress was about to set a bad precedent; for if it could pass a law abridging the freedom of the press, might it not be asked to pass a law against the circulation of pamphlets on political and religious subjects?[82] He protested against the right of persons to examine parcels put in the post office, for that was seizure and search which was denied in every civilized country. Without this the postmaster would have no way of knowing what was in the mail. He also argued that whenever a parcel was placed in the mail it became the property of the person to whom it was addressed and was not subject to destruction by anyone, certainly not by the Deputy Postmaster.[83] He closed his argument by insisting that such a bill, if passed, would destroy the freedom of the press.

Another who spoke against this bill was Henry Clay of Kentucky. He opposed the bill also because it was indefinite and might apply to papers then in operation or to any future papers or material which touched slavery. He felt that the bill was uncalled for by public sentiment and that it was unconstitutional and dangerous to the liberties of the people.[84] He said further that Congress could pass no law that would prohibit these papers from the mail. In this view he differed from both Buchanan and Calhoun. He felt that the transportation of the mail was not the harmful thing, but rather the circulation in the states.[85] The remedy was in the hands of the states and not of the National Government, he contended. The bill was too general in its application, applying, as it stood, to the non-slaveholding states. The proposed law had decreed that the postmaster must not violate it

[81] G. T. Curtis, *Life of James Buchanan*, I, 339.
[82] Gales and Seaton, *Register of Debates*, XII, part 2, 1721.
[83] G. T. Curtis, *Life of James Buchanan*, I, 340.
[84] Carl Schurz, *Life of Henry Clay*, American Statesmen Series, II, 84.
[85] *Globe*, Appendix, 24th Congress, 1st Session, 439.

knowingly. In order to be exempt from this law all the post-master need do was to claim ignorance, and thus protect himself from the penalties under the law.[86] Kendall had pointed out to the postmasters that to open the mail was unlawful and that to do so would be their own responsibility; they could not expect protection from the general post office. The law regulating the post office had not given to the postmasters the power to know the contents of the mail.[87] Clay had followed, in his attack upon the bill, much the same reasoning as had Davis of Massachusetts.

Morris of Ohio opposed the bill because it made the law of Congress subject to the laws of twenty-four states; this arrangement he considered an error. He thought that when a person subscribed for a paper and paid the postage on it, it belonged to the subscriber and any interference was a violation of the Constitution.[88] He had no fear of the constant threat of disunion by the southern representatives, for he was certain it could never be carried into effect.

The last opposition to be noticed here is the objection of Thomas Hart Benton of Missouri. Benton opposed the bill because of its far-reaching extent. He did not want to make a pack horse out of the National Government but thought it was going quite a distance to clothe 10,000 postmasters with the power proposed under the bill. He insisted that he hated to vote against a measure which seemed even in appearance to have for its object the suppression of the evil complained of by the southern states.[89] Benton's attitude had to be explained, for Missouri had passed a law against incendiary papers and no doubt expected her representatives to support any measure which had for its purpose the suppression of the evil.

The bill as reported by Calhoun was debated pro and con until July 2, 1836. On that day, when it was called up for consideration, Grundy moved to amend the bill by striking out all after the enacting clause and substituting three new sections.[90] The arguments which had been directed against the bill had shown that the bill was too comprehensive and forced the postmasters to know the laws of all the states. Grundy's substitution made it unlawful for any postmaster knowingly to deliver to any

[86] G. T. Curtis, *James Buchanan*, I, 348.
[87] Amos Kendall, *Autobiography*, 648.
[88] Morris, *Life of Morris*, 289.
[89] T. H. Benton, *Abridgment of Debates in Congress*, XII, 759.
[90] *Globe*, 24th Congress, 1st Session, III, 416.

person any material touching the subject of slavery where the circulation was prohibited. The penalty for violation of this act was removal forthwith from office.[91] This section transferred the responsibility from the sending to the receiving office and removed the fines which were in the original bill The second section said that nothing in the act of Congress to establish and regulate the Post Office Department should be construed to protect the postmaster who would violate the first section of this amended bill. The receiving office was to give notice to the person or persons sending the papers and give them a chance to withdraw their papers. If this request had not been complied with in a month, the papers were to be burned or otherwise destroyed.[92]

The Grundy substitute was much simpler than the original bill from the point of view of the postmaster, for all he needed to do was to familiarize himself with the laws of his own state and comply with the proposed measure. He could comply with the existing law and practice of the National Government which had decreed that the papers must be sent. This proposed amendment destroyed one of the most forceful arguments advanced against the bill, namely, that it punished one postmaster for not doing what it forced another to do; now every one had to do the same thing. The postmasters in the North had no choice in the matter of circulating abolition literature under this measure; they must send it.

This controversy in the Senate was over the authority of the state to control by its police power the action of the Federal Government. It is not surprising that the question caused a difference of opinion at such an early day; for it is not clear now just how far the states may interfere with the mails.[93]

Calhoun tried to amend Grundy's substitute so that when the papers were sent to a state where they were prohibited by the laws of that State a requisition would be made upon the postal authorities to deliver them to a person or persons appointed to receive them.[94] These persons were to burn them or otherwise dispose of them under the regulation of the Post Office Department. This amendment was supported by a strict sectional vote; Clay of Kentucky and Goldsborough of Maryland were the only Senators in the border states who voted for the Calhoun amend-

[91] *Ibid.*, 437.
[92] *Globe*, 24th Congress, 1st Session, III, 416. This, like the first proposed bill, made the laws of the states paramount. It was a "States' Rights" bill.
[93] Lindsay, *Postal Powers of Congress*, Johns Hopkins Studies, 24.
[94] T. H. Benton, *Abridgment of Debates in Congress*, XII, 771.

ment. The other supporters were from the strictly southern states. Every Senator who opposed the bill came from the northern states or from a border state.[95] We find some of the Jacksonian Democrats and also some Whigs casting their votes with Calhoun. The party lines would not hold and the vote was a tie. Being in the committee of the whole, the Vice President, Van Buren, the most prominent Democratic candidate for the presidency, did not vote for the measure.[96] The Grundy substitution was concurred in and that substitute took the place of Calhoun's bill.[97] When this substitute came up for engrossment and the third reading on the same day, June 2, another tie vote developed. The vote was not as much a sectional one as the one on the Calhoun amendment, for three northern Senators voted for engrossment. Buchanan of Pennsylvania, Wright and Tallmadge of New York supported the bill for engrossment, and were all Democrats who voted for the bill; most of those who voted for it from the South were Democrats save Hugh White, who had by this time gone over to the side of the Whig party. He was the only prominent Whig who voted for the measure. These Democrats who voted for the bill did not vote as to leadership, as Calhoun Democrats or as Jacksonian Democrats. All the prominent Whigs and some of the Democrats voted against the measure. It can hardly be called a party vote; it was rather a sectional one.[98] There was a political move in this vote, according to T. H. Benton. He accuses Calhoun of arranging the tie so that Van Buren would have to vote on the question and thus show the South his attitude toward this important subject.[99] Van Buren assumed the responsibility and voted for the engrossment of the measure.[100] Benton also thought Wright voted politically. He was a political and personal friend of Van Buren and furnished the best index of the Vice President's opinion.[101] The bill was now engrossed by the narrow margin of one vote and put upon its final passage.

The bill was called up for final passage on June 8 by Calhoun. The vote was taken and the bill was lost 19 to 25. The vote on the passage of the bill became a sectional one more so than the others; the New York Senators and Buchanan voted for the

[95] *Globe*, 24th Congress, 1st Session, III, 416.
[96] T. H. Benton, *Thirty Years' View*, I, 587.
[97] *Globe*, 24th Congress, 1st Session, III, 416. Eighteen Senators were absent on Calhoun's amendment; twelve on Grundy's amendment.
[98] T. H. Benton, *Abridgment of Debates in Congress*, XII, 771.
[99] T. H. Benton, *Thirty Years' View*, I, 587.
[100] E. M. Shepherd, *Martin Van Buren*, American Statesmen Series, 237.
[101] T. H. Benton, *Thirty Years' View*, I, 587.

measure, but the Maryland Senators voted against it.[102] There was scarcely any semblance of party lines in the vote. Mangum, a Whig, voted for the measure; and the Maryland Senators, one a Whig and one a Democrat, voted against the measure. Robinson of Illinois voted for the measure, while Benton of Missouri voted against it. Benton insisted that he voted against the measure because he had grown tired of the eternal cry of the dissolution of the Union.[103] This brought to a close in the Senate this controversy over abolition papers and other material. The Senate had definitely decided to pass no law that might be considered and abridgment of the freedom of speech. That this bill was considered a political one is well expressed by Seward, who said no one could hope to gain the North who gave his support to a bill so destructive to the interest of the North and expressed the hope that Van Buren's men would not support such a measure.[104]

The House held the controversy of the circulation of abolition literature to its regular committee and thus it did not lead to the confusion and strife there which it caused in the Senate. The Committee on Post Offices and Post Roads in the House reported a bill to reorganize the Post Office which the Postmaster-General had recommended. The bill contained forty-six sections and went into minute details in regulating the Post Office.[105] The thirty-second section had to do with the question of antislavery literature. This law made it unlawful for any deputy postmaster to retain any literature or give preference to one pamphlet over another. This bill seems to be directly opposed to what the South wanted, but careful analysis will show it gave the South the same thing as the Grundy substitution had promised except that it made no provision for disposing of the papers when they reached their destination.[106] The bill said that the papers must be sent to their destination, which was exactly what the Grundy substitution said. The Grundy bill said they must not be delivered where they were prohibited by the laws of the states and the Post Office law made no mention of this matter. This had been cared for and the papers could not be delivered in a single southern state, whatever the law of the United States was. This closed the contest in the Congress of the United States.

[102] Globe, 24th Congress, 1st Session, 418.
[103] T. H. Benton, Thirty Years' View, I, 588.
[104] W. H. Seward, Autobiography, I, 293.
[105] Statutes at Large, V, 80.
[106] Ibid.

CHAPTER VI

THE POLITICAL IMPORTANCE OF THE ABOLITION CONTROVERSY

The controversy over the distribution of anti-slavery papers came at a time when the political situation had created a bitter contest. The Whigs were making an effort to displace the Democrats and overthrow the Jackson reign. The Whig party had been without the service of a leader that was able to make much headway against Jackson's popularity.[1] The Democratic party was lessening its chances for success by splitting into two factions, one the Jacksonian and the other the Calhoun Democrats. The Calhounites liked to think of themselves as members of no party, since they were not allied at that time with any party with national significance.[2] They were opposed to Jackson and stood solidly for the policy of Calhoun. In 1835 Calhoun was making an effort to overthrow the influence of Jackson and defeat Van Buren for the presidency. The slavery question which came into prominence in 1835 offered just the opportunity which was needed. The test of party loyalty was to be found in the attitude of that party toward the slave question.

It was not a fear of the distribution of these papers which caused so much excitement in the South. Calhoun said in the course of debate on the anti-slavery petitions January 7, "Sir, we fear not the incendiary publications in the South." The South, he felt, was too well aware of what was due it, to allow the circulation of those pamphlets there. He feared circulation would cause the southern press to discuss the matter in the presence of slaves.[3] Black of Mississippi said the abolition papers were not circulated in the South; they could not be circulated there, for they could not enlighten the South.[4] If, then, as these spokesmen of the South claimed, the papers could not circulate there, the

---

[1] James Schouler, *History of the United States of America*, IV, 192.
[2] *Ibid.*, 193.
[3] *Congressional Globe*, 24th Congress, 1st Session, III, 77.
[4] Gales and Seaton, *Register of Debates*, XII, Part I, 650.

real controversy was not over the distribution of abolition literature. The motive for the activity of certain leaders in the South
was a political one. Judge Story in describing the political situation of the period said that upon political questions men were
blind, deaf, and dumb.[5] This in a way explains the attempt to tie
up the slavery question with political activities; the purpose was
to befuddle the average voter and confuse the issues.

The *Mobile Commercial Register* asked who were the accomplices of the abolitionists, the Northern Whigs or the friends of
Van Buren. The editor said, if he was not mistaken, the ninety-
nine administration members of Congress had remained opposed
to abolition in every form. On the motion to print the memorials
in the House, only eight of the ninety-nine administration members voted to print, while the Whigs as a whole from the non-
slaveholding states voted to print. This fact the editor took as an
indictment against the Whigs and thus allied them with the abolitionist.[6] This same paper spoke out earlier against the Whig
party and blamed the members of this party for trying to stir up
and exasperate the passion of brother against brother. But the
real design of the Whigs, it said, was to direct public attention
from the course of Dr. Leigh, to defeat the election of Van Buren,
get in Webster or Clay, dissolve the Union, and then make John
C. Calhoun dictator, King, or Emperor of all that section which
had the Potomac on the north and the Mississippi on the west.[7]
The *Richmond Enquirer* blamed the Whigs for connecting the
Democrats with the activities of the abolitionist.[8] The article considered it only a political trick to discredit the Democrats. There
was an attempt to connect the States' Right party with the abolitionist. They were accused of doing this for the dissolution of
the Union. Thus the *Savannah Republican* considered it a political
trick and denounced those who were responsible for that rumor.[9]
The *Richmond Enquirer* blamed Duff Green and his kind for trying to use the fanatics to break up the Union and prevent the elec-

[5] W. W. Story, *Life of Joseph Story*, II, 49. Letter to Professor Ashum
of Banger Theological Seminary.

[6] January 4, 1836. Massachusetts, twelve Whigs; Vermont, five Whigs.
Vermont's five Whigs all voted for printing the abolition petitions. In New
York eight Whigs out of nine voted for printing. This the editor took as
proof that the Whigs were in favor of the abolitionist.

[7] *Ibid.*, August 19, 1835.

[8] *Richmond Enquirer*, July 24, 1835.

[9] *Savannah Republican*, August 10, 1835.

tion of Van Buren.[10] It was a common trick for one party to try to align the other party with the abolitionist. The reason for this is very clear. The South would have nothing to do with any party which ignored the interests of the South, and this was the reason why so much effort was put forth on the part of the papers to connect the opposite party with the abolitionist.

The South was wrought up over the slave question and especially over the circulation of these objectionable papers. A New York gentleman traveling in Georgia, who did not give his name, said the fanatics had almost broken up travelling in the South. Only those who were rich and well known could travel there. He felt sure the people of Georgia were so wrought up that Van Buren would lose Georgia.[11] The Huntsville, Alabama, *Advocate* said of the South and its political intentions that the section would not join the West in the support of Harrison, nor would it join the North in the election of Webster.[12]

In Virginia the legislature took up the question of anti-slavery papers. The method proposed was to correspond with the non-slaveholding states, to ascertain what laws had been passed to regulate these abolition societies. The resolution was defeated almost along party lines.[13] This was construed by the Democrats as a political trick on the part of the Whigs to keep up the agitation. The Whigs claimed it embraced the will of the people.[14] The question of slavery colored all party movements and activities.

The Calhoun Democrats were making an effort to bring the South together on the question of slavery, as the other issues had failed. Economic policy had not done so, for different sections could not agree upon any particular issue. The railroad question was looked upon as an issue, which would bind the South together, but local interests killed that. As a result, all parties turned to make the slavery question a paramount issue upon which the South could be successfully united. Thomas Cooper in a letter to J. H. Hammond on January 8, 1836, said, ''Even upon the slave

[10] *Mobile Commercial Register*, August 10, 1836.

[11] *Savannah Republican*, September 21, 1835. This prophecy proved true, for Van Buren did lose that state. *Cyclopedia of Political Science, Political Economy and United States History*, II, 57.

[12] *Cincinnati Gazette*, October 21, 1835.

[13] H. H. Simms, *Rise of Whig Party in Virginia*, 103.

[14] *Ibid.*, 104. A bill did pass, however. It was agreed that the northern states would be called upon for penal laws. There was a fear that it might hurt Van Buren's chances for the Presidency.

question you cannot depend upon the southern Van Buren member.''[15]

The *Richmond Whig* claimed that the South was determined to cease not, to tire not until their rights were granted to them by an act of Congress. The act which was called for must not be a doubtful one, but must be clear, strong, and unequivocal. The South was asked to stick together on this question; and if the North, in the majority, passed a law opposed to the southern interests, then Van Buren would lose all chances of an election. Those might be chosen to vote who were most popular at home, but in any case the South must win in this slavery contest. Van Buren in order to win the South must go with that section or send some of his faithful lieutenants to carry the day for the South.[16] Seward did not see how the abolition question could hurt in any way than to drive the South to the support of a southern man. Whatever was done in the North would not be sufficient to break the spell of Jackson.[17] Seward thought that if Van Buren should lose most of the South, he would still win, but the loss of the North would be disastrous to his cause.

Van Buren was a northern man, so that it was an easy matter for the opposition to say that he was opposed to the interest of the South. It was very difficult to hold the support for Van Buren. Richard E. Parker wrote Van Buren on August 21, 1835, reminding him that much feeling was being displayed over the anti-slavery agitation. He feared that the Whig party would win this favorable sentiment to its advantage unless the Democrats made a positive statement.[18] The papers, he said, talked about the natural rights of the slave to emancipate himself. This was a very objectionable doctrine from the point of view of the South, and Parker could see what danger this would be, coming from the northern section. It would be an easy matter to make the mass of the southern voters believe that Van Buren supported such views.

Governor William Schley of Georgia wrote to Van Buren on August 22, 1835, to relate to him the importance of some definite expression against the abolitionist. The citizens of that section, he said, were so incensed that unless the people of the North, the

[15] *J. H. Hammond Papers*, V. Letter of January 8, 1836. He was writing in reference to petitions. Cooper, President of the College of South Carolina.

[16] *Richmond Whig and Public Advertiser*, January 14, 1836.

[17] W. H. Seward, *Autobiography*, I, 293.

[18] Van Buren MSS., XXII. Letter to Van Buren.

great majority of whom professed to be opposed to the schemes and plans of these incendiaries, did something in the way of legislation to put the abolitionist down the consequences might be fatal to the Union and to the present administration and its friends. The enemies of the administration impressed upon the people the idea that these people were in fact speaking the mad sentiments of the whole North and that Van Buren was in favor of abolishing slavery and would use his power for that purpose if he were elected. Schley reminded Van Buren as the representative of the great Union Republican party of the United States that it would be necessary for New York to pass some type of legislation in order to keep those opposed to Van Buren from using that as an argument against him and his party. The Republican party in the South could give no answer to the question when asked why Van Buren and his friends, if opposed, did not pass laws to punish the abolitionist. The governor said everyone had a right to expect such a provision from the Republican party of New York, and such a course would secure the votes of the South for Van Buren. It would also, he thought, put down those who sought to dissolve the Union and use the excitement over slavery to effect their treasonable designs.[19] This long letter explained the condition of the party in Georgia in the late summer of 1835.

At this time, there was much excitement in various parts of the state of Virginia, especially around Mecklenburg, over the question of the abolition of slavery. Richard Baptist from Mecklenburg County wrote to Van Buren that the salvation of the party in that section depended upon a denunciation of the abolition party. This must be given wide circulation in the country.[20] He was gratified that the sentiment expressed at several public meetings was favorable. These public meetings mentioned were those held in the North immediately after the excitement at Charleston, condemning the abolition societies. Van Buren had given his views on these questions as early as 1834. He said his opinions were so well known in the South that he was surprised that anyone should attempt to deceive the public regarding them. The subject of slavery was exclusively under the control of the state, he said, and he did not see how the general government could interfere without a change in the Constitution.[21]

[19] *Van Buren Papers*, XXII; to Van Buren written from Athens, Georgia, August 22, 1835.
[20] *Ibid.*, letter of September 2, 1835.
[21] *Ibid.*, XXIII, letter to Samuel Gwin from Van Buren, July 11, 1824.

In spite of this clear explanation, the statement was not sufficient for several of the leading party members and the southern public. James B. Mallory wrote to Van Buren to say that his opinion of the power of Congress over the state was perfectly satisfactory, but a better explanation of the power of Congress over the District of Columbia was desired.[22] W. A. Gillespie of Louisa County, Virginia, wrote to Van Buren for an explanation of the power of Congress over the District of Columbia. He was not satisfied with Van Buren's explanation of the power of Congress in the District. He asked Van Buren if Congress had the power to destroy private property unless it was put to public use and if the state could abolish slavery without paying the master.[23] M. Blakely of Depot, North Carolina, wrote the same views. He wanted an expression from Van Buren in order that all barriers might be out of the way in his election. He wanted to know definitely if Van Buren opposed abolition activities.[24] These many requests show how important the action of Van Buren was considered in party circles.

Van Buren wrote a letter on September 10, 1835, in which, like his letter in 1834 to Samuel Gwin, in Mississippi, he denied that Congress had any right to interfere with slavery in the District of Columbia.[25] This question became so important that in March, 1836, he published his reply in the form of a political pamphlet so there could be little doubt of his position. He took the same attitude that the Albany convention had expressed as his attitude on the anti-slavery papers, which were flooding the country. This convention had been called together by the leading citizens of that city, and had condemned the abolition societies.[26] Those who were in charge of that meeting were friends of Van Buren and therefore spoke his sentiments. It was easy for him to use the resolutions of that meeting as his opinion on the anti-slavery papers.

On the question of the power of Congress over slavery in the District of Columbia he gave a long explanation and finally came to the conclusion that slavery in the District was exclusively un-

---

[22] *Van Buren Papers*, XXIII, letter of March 5, 1836.
[23] *Ibid.*, letter of April 13, 1836.
[24] *Ibid.*, letter of September 6, 1835.
[25] Letter was written in Awasco, New York. The letter does not state to whom it was written. It was printed in the *Augusta Courier*, September 10, 1835.
[26] *Niles Register*, XLIX, 28. This meeting was held September 4, 1835, and was called to order by Governor Marcy.

der the control of Congress. He realized the importance of his
answer upon the political situation and hastened to say that he
was ready to change if he were shown to be in error. Van Buren
said that if he were elevated to the presidency he would be an
inflexible and uncompromising opponent of any attempt on the
part of Congress to abolish slavery in the District of Columbia
against the wishes of the slaveholding states.[27] The *Southern
Patriot* said that Van Buren's idea of the power of Congress over
slavery in the District of Columbia was that the abolition of
slavery would be contrary to the laws of Maryland and Virginia.[28]
This is the doctrine which was emphasized in the Compromise
of 1850.

Not only was Van Buren called upon to answer for the attitude of the Democratic party, but also his party leaders were
forced to express themselves. B. F. Butler, Attorney-General of
the United States, wrote to Hugh A. Garland, Mecklenburg, Virginia, concerning Van Buren's opinion.[29] He gave nothing new
and showed himself the true politician by attempting to cloud the
issue. Senator Silas Wright, from New York, wrote to Thomas
Ritchie, editor of the *Enquirer,* concerning Van Buren's views
and said that he was glad to answer the question which had been
sent to him by Ritchie for the benefit of the administration members of the Virginia Legislature. The question was whether Van
Buren thought Congress had the power to abolish slavery in the
District of Columbia and whether Congress had the right to interfere with the relation of master and slave in any of the states.
The Senator said that his relation to Van Buren enabled him to
answer with assurance and without reserve. He thought that the
Constitution of the United States did not, in the opinion of Van
Buren, give Congress the right to interfere with the relations be-
tween master and slave in any of the states, and would think it
impolitic for that body to pass a law abolishing slavery in the
District of Columbia.[30]

This question of slavery was important to the Democratic party
and gave much concern. A Democratic convention was held at
Fredericksburg on July 4, 1836. The delegates from adjacent
counties had met for the purpose of sending forth an address to

[27] *Van Buren Papers,* XXIII. He gave his answers largely in the papers
and in pamphlets.
[28] *Southern Patriot,* March 24, 1836.
[29] *Van Buren Papers,* XXIII.
[30] *Ibid.,* XXII. Published originally in the *Enquirer.*

the Democratic party in Virginia. This was necessary because the party was in need of an explanation of Van Buren's attitude. In the proceedings of the convention the participants said that they had hoped that the recent casting vote of Van Buren on the subject of incendiary publications would silence the futile and ridiculous charge of his being an abolitionist and would prove his frankness to his enemies.[31]

The question of whether Van Buren was an abolitionist or not kept constantly making its appearance in one way or another. The reason was, in spite of the fact that Van Buren was chosen by Jackson, the South was not satisfied with his vote in the legislature of New York on matters relating to slavery. In 1820 Van Buren had voted against a resolution favoring the entrance of Missouri into the Union with her slaves, when the matter came before the legislature of that state. Van Buren explained his action by the fact that Governor Clinton had asked in his annual message that the entrance of Missouri be opposed.[32] This was not satisfactory to the South. The *Columbus Georgia Enquirer* dug up a letter written by Van Buren in 1819 to a friend. It said, "I should regret to feel any flagging on the subject of Mr. King. We are submitted to his support. It is honest, and we must have no fluttering in our course. Mr. King's views toward us are both honest and correct. The Missouri question conceals, so far as he is concerned, no plot, and we shall give it a true direction. You know what the feelings and views of our friends were when I saw you; and you know what we then concluded to do, etc., and the aspect of the *Argus* will show you that we have entered on the work in earnest. We cannot, therefore, look back. Let us not, therefore, have any halting."[33] Whatever explanation was given, the South could not help asking for assurance that Van Buren would be faithful to its interests. There was still another charge which the South had against Van Buren; that was, he had voted in the New York State Constitutional Convention to allow Negroes who paid taxes to vote. The motion which Van Buren was concerned about was to strike out the word "white," which meant blacks and whites were allowed to vote, and he voted for the motion.[34] If the word "white" had been inserted it would have excluded all Negroes but when the

---

[31] *Van Buren Papers*, XXII.
[32] *Niles Register*, XLIX, 141.
[33] *Niles Register*, XLIX, 93. Quoted from *Augusta Courier*.
[34] *Ibid.*, 132. The vote was passed 63 to 56.

word "black" was inserted it gave all Negroes who paid taxes the right to vote. This was Van Buren's record, and it kept him constantly trying to explain his attitude to the South. It probably made a difference in Van Buren's action. Van Buren might have been expected to have voted against the engrossment of the bill to regulate abolition literature, for his section was opposed to it; but when there was a tie vote, he voted for its engrossment and made himself solid with the South. Much of this action was for political purpose.

The Whig party was accused also of making much out this abolitionist matter in a political way. James Barbour wrote to Henry Clay on August 2, 1835, and gave his opinions of the Whig party in Virginia. He said the Whigs had generally decided to support White as their candidate. He thought if only a small accession from the Jackson ranks could be secured, it might give enough power to control the state. However, he thought this could not be done, for the Jackson Democrats had been told the Whigs were playing false, that they wished to divide the Jacksonians so as to bring the election into the House and elect either Clay or Webster or some other prominent Whig.[35] The Whig party of the South was the party of the slaveholder because it was the party which had in its ranks a considerable majority of the large cotton, tobacco, rice, and sugar planters.[36] It was only natural that any claim that it was connected with abolitionists was denied vigorously.

John Rankin, of Ohio, advised the abolition members to support the Whig party because they would profit more by that than they would by supporting the Democrats. His reason for asking for the support of the Whigs was that the Whigs were much weaker, he thought, and since one party was to be in power it was the duty of the abolitionist to help that party from whom they could get most good. It was evident that this question had much to do with the political situation in 1836. There were several efforts to link first one party and then the other with the abolition crusade. It was evident that no party could be elected which supported the abolitionists. The circulation of the first abolitionist papers brought this matter into the field of politics. It was a troublesome proposition for Van Buren, but it could hardly prevent his election because of his support by Jackson.

[35] Clay's *Works*, edited by C. Colter, V, 397.
[36] A. C. Cole, *The Whig Party in the South*, 204. The Whig party was preëminently, though not exclusively, the slaveholders' party.

Chapter VII

THE CONTEST FROM 1836 TO 1840

The contest which had begun in 1835, when the abolitionists had announced their new program, had not culminated in June, 1836, at which time Congress passed the post office bill which laid down the policy of the United States in reference to the distribution of mails and other materials placed in the post office. The question arises: Did the South abide by this law and distribute what was sent to it, or did it enforce its own local laws in spite of the laws of Congress? These are important questions and must be considered. It is convenient to divide the period from 1836 to 1860 into two parts: from 1836 to 1840, and from 1840 to 1860. These divisions appear natural because of events which happened.

The abolition societies were not unmindful of the importance of this controversy over the use of the mail as an aid in their cause, for in 1836 the Massachusetts Anti-Slavery Society said in its fourth annual report that the affair in Charleston had lighted a fire which would not go out until slavery was removed from the continent of North America.[1] This same report said that the people of Massachusetts were sure that the axe had been laid at the root of the tree because of the many events which had happened.[2] The Massachusetts society was glad to say in its next report that the mouths of the abolitionists had not been closed, but unmolested freedom of speech and untrammelled freedom of the press on the subject of slavery were everywhere denied them.[3] The abolitionists spoke and printed during this period not only at the risk of their reputations, but of their lives, the Society thought. In spite of the fact that no law had been passed by Congress which would hinder them, the abolitionists realized that they spoke at great peril.

[1] Massachusetts Anti-Slavery Society, *Fourth Annual Report*, 1836.
[2] Massachusetts Anti-Slavery Society, *Fourth Annual Report*, 1836, 8.
[3] *Ibid., Fifth Annual Report*, 5.

The fourth annual report of the American Anti-Slavery Society said the press was free, guarded by the state and the nation, and it could discuss anything other than the wrongs of slavery. The report considered as a great wrong the license given mobs by public opinion.[4] It had been thought presumptuous to discuss the freedom of the press, and the Constitution had been nullified. The society went on with its work in spite of the attitude of the public. This same report showed that there had been organized during the year 1837, 483 societies, making 1,006 societies which were flourishing. The publications had not increased, but a large number of these papers were being printed. During the period covered by this report, 787 bound volumes were printed, 47,250 tracts and pamphlets, 4,100 circulars, 10,490 prints, 900 *Anti-Slavery Magazines*, 130,150 *Slaves' Friends*, 103,000 *Anti-Slavery Records*, 189,400 *Human Rights*, and 217,080 *Emancipators*, which show that the society had not neglected its publications.[5] The year of 1838 saw a decrease in the publications. The total number in that year was 646,502. The reason for this decrease may be explained by the change in the policy of the organization, which now turned much more of its attention to the living agent.[6] However, there was a large number of those papers being sent and still more being founded. The problem had not been settled for the reason that the societies were determined to send their publications, and the South was determined to prohibit them.

The controversy over the mail and the press raged throughout this period. The *Philanthropist* was established by James G. Birney, a native of Kentucky, whose father was reputed to be one of the wealthiest men in the state, and who had all the advantages which wealth could give.[7] He was a firm believer in gradual emancipation and one of the most active members in that organization which had been established to diminish slavery by degrees. His progress from a gradual to immediate abolition was slow. By 1836, the society for the gradual emancipation had been abolished, and James G. Birney had to seek a new association, especially because he had begun to realize now that gradual emancipation was of little value. On March 19, 1835, he or-

[4] American Anti-Slavery Society, *Fourth Annual Report*, 113.
[5] American Anti-Slavery Society, *Fourth Annual Report*, 31. The total number for this year was 711, 277.
[6] *Ibid., Fifth Annual Report*, 1838, 48.
[7] W. Birney, *James G. Birney and His Times*, 14.

ganized in his own home town, Danville, an auxiliary to the American Anti-Slavery Society.[8]

By 1835 Birney had become a national figure because of his outspoken expression and because he had freed his own slaves. He decided to publish a paper in Kentucky which he titled *The Philanthropist,* and called a mass meeting at Danville for the purpose of a discussion of the proposed plan. Resolutions were passed, and those present pledged themselves to put a stop to his plan and to use any means necessary, peaceful or forceful, to prevent the publication of the *Philanthropist.*[9] A committee, which was appointed at this meeting, wrote Birney on July 12, 1835, and demanded that he cease to publish his proposed paper until an appeal could be made to the legislature. The uncompromising Birney, of course, did not comply with the demand, for he considered the freedom of the press one of the most precious and inalienable rights.[10] Birney realized, as everyone did, the inherent difficulties that were to be met by starting a paper in a slaveholding state. He wrote Gerrit Smith, a prominent abolitionist in New York, that he feared the project would probably not go through; but if it did, the paper would be out about July 15. The publisher of Birney's proposed paper was bribed by his opponents and would not print the paper for him; thus he realized his usefulness in Kentucky was over.[11] This was about the time of the great excitement over the mail in all parts of the South; so Birney was doubtful if he could use the mail and thought it would be advisable for him to leave Kentucky and move to Ohio where the laws were conducive to his work. The editor of *The Liberator* thought that Birney showed little judgment in starting an anti-slavery paper in a slave state. He called it an attempt to talk anti-slavery in a den of lions. The editorial said that if Birney should find himself minus his head the day after he published his paper he would have only himself to blame.[12] He did not lose his head; for he did not publish the paper.

The Cincinnati papers gave plenty of publicity to the matter. One stated that James G. Birney was about to start an abo-

---

[8] A. E. Martin, *Anti-Slavery Movement in Kentucky Prior to 1850,* 74.
[9] *Ibid.,* 180.
[10] *Ibid.,* 181. The committee appointed by the citizens consisted of 33 persons.
[11] A. E. Martin, *Anti-Slavery Movement in Kentucky Prior to 1840,* 183. Extract from Smith's letter, Birney's book.
[12] *The Liberator,* August 15, 1835.

lition paper near the city after having failed in both Danville and Cincinnati, and insisted that the establishment of such a paper was an insult to the slaveholding states.[13] The *Cincinnati Republic* was also outspoken in denouncing Birney. In spite of this opposition Birney went on with his work, and the paper was published at New Richmond. The paper was so well edited and so moderate in tone that it disarmed all opposition.[14] The paper was very mild, and even conducted a slaveholder's column. The writer in one number said that he would recommend to the consideration of the legislature a revision of existing laws, so as to prevent more effectively the circulation through the post office of any publications tending to endanger domestic relations.[15] It discussed the general topics of the day along with the slave question.

Birney, misled by the subsiding of the violent opposition, moved his paper to Cincinnati. He was mistaken, for those who had opposed him still continued to do so.[16] Things went along quietly for a while, and although the pro-slavery feeling was running high, there was no demonstration. The subscription list of *The Philanthropist* was 1,700 and still increasing. This was a large subscription for an anti-slavery paper at that early time.[17]

Opposition to Birney soon broke out again. On July 12, 1836, at midnight a band of about thirty men, including those who stood as sentinels, scaled the walls, entered the building by means of an open window, descended to the press room, tore up that week's edition of the paper, destroyed the ink, and carried away part of the press.[18] Coffin thought those who took part in this affair were men of worth in the community and not a mere mob.

There was much hostility toward Birney, as was shown by a meeting held in Cincinnati in January, when Birney was first allowed to speak and then was silenced.[19] This was at an anti-slavery meeting which showed the hostility that was evident toward slavery. It was due only to the influence of Charles Ham-

---

[13] *Cincinnati Whig*, December 21, 1835.
[14] H. Wilson, *Rise and Fall of Slave Power*, I, 276.
[15] *The Philanthropist*, January 15, 1836. This number was published at New Richmond.
[16] *Ibid., James G. Birney and His Times*, 240; the paper was moved to Cincinnati April, 1836.
[17] Levi Coffin, *Reminiscences*, 524. *The Philanthropist* was the organ of the Ohio Anti-Slavery Society.
[18] Levi Coffin, *op. cit.*, 525.
[19] *Cincinnati Daily Gazette*, January 27, 1836.

mond, editor of the *Daily Gazette*, that Birney was allowed to remain in Cincinnati at all.[20]

Birney, after his paper had been destroyed, appealed to the mayor of the city to issue a proclamation and to offer a reward for the apprehension of the person or persons responsible for the destruction of his property. The one which was issued was not calculated to impress the lawless citizens that the mayor was sincere.[21] *The Philanthropist*, through the mayor, offered $100 as a reward for the capture of those responsible for the disturbance. This affair did not disturb Birney; he kept on printing his paper, and it came out as usual.

This action of Birney's was not satisfactory to the anti-abolitionist party; popular excitement existed in the city, and placards were posted on the corners of the streets warning the abolition society to beware. Several of the city papers expressed the same idea only in more guarded language.[22] These acts tended to increase the excitement instead of decreasing it. From July 18, to July 24 various articles and editorials appeared in the papers condemning the abolitionist. There appeared an anonymous advertisement in the papers calling a meeting in the town market on July 23, at six o'clock.[23] The purpose of the meeting, as set forth in the hand-bills and in the notice in the papers, was to determine whether the paper was to be allowed to be printed in Cincinnati or not. The meeting convened at the appointed time and passed resolutions condemning the action of Birney and his associates as detrimental to the welfare of the city and at variance with the opinion of the sister states.[24] At the time the resolutions were passed it was agreed to send Birney a request to cease the publication of his paper, and he was warned further that if the abolition society insisted upon the publication, the people of Cincinnati could not be responsible for what happened because of the tense feeling in the city.[25] The reason this was asked was that it was said it would ruin the trade and the property interests of the city.[26] Another who lived in Cincinnati

[20] G. H. Payne, *History of Journalism in the United States*, 227.
[21] Birney, *James G. Birney and His Times*, 242; *Niles Register*, L, 397. The mayor would not issue a proclamation until the money was deposited.
[22] Levi Coffin, *op. cit.*, 525.
[23] Birney, *op. cit.*, 243.
[24] *Niles Register*, L, 297. The committee decided not only to put down the *Philanthropist* but to put down any paper of a similar nature.
[25] *Niles Register*, L, 298.
[26] W. H. Smith, *Charles Hammond*, 60.

they turned their attention to the Negroes and tore down some of their houses.[33]

This violence in Cincinnati linked the question of slavery with the freedom of the press which the Constitution and the laws of Ohio had guaranteed. The Birney riot brought others to the rescue of this fundamental right. This action led Salmon P. Chase to a realization of the importance of the slave question. He decided to give it serious consideration, although he was not an abolitionist.[34] It was rumored that Chase said he would give $10,000 to support an abolitionist press. This caused some concern, and thus he wrote an article to explain what he actually did say. He explained that he would give $10,000 rather than see any press destroyed by mob violence, however obnoxious it might be. He expressed his abhorrence of mob violence and explained that he intended to support the press, whatever the grievance in a lawful way.[35] Another in this same class with Chase was John Rankin, one of the most prominent citizens of Ohio, who continued the condemnation which he had begun before this time.

After the Birney riot Charles Hammond called together a meeting which was taken over by the slavery forces, and all he could do was to publish his protest.[36] He insisted that slavery was a domestic institution and belonged exclusively to the state where it was found and that no state had a right to interfere with it. While he agreed to this doctrine, he could not see the Constitution and laws trampled in the dust. This right, the petition stated, was the bulwark of all the rest; namely, the right of free discussion, and the right of every citizen to write, speak, and print upon any subject he thought proper.[37] Hammond rested his case upon the law.

Another person wrote anonymously in the *Gazette* but hastened to let it be known that he was not an abolitionist. He said that the confusion which had been going on in the city in the last few days was due to the contest over the freedom of speech and the press. The writer thought the right was too sacred to be given to any mob and that every free man should attack those

[33] Birney, *op. cit.*, 247. Extract from the *Cincinnati Gazette*, August 1, 1835.

[34] A. B. Hart, *Salmon P. Chase, American Statesmen Series*, XXVIII, 51.

[35] *Chase Papers*, in Library of Congress, III, 1836-37. Printed in the *Cincinnati Gazette*, August 4, 1836.

[36] W. N. Smith, *op. cit.*, 61.

[37] W. H. Smith, *op. cit.*, 62. Principle laid down in Giddings' resolutions later.

who would destroy that right.[38]   It was not the destruction of *The Philanthropist* that was significant but the attack upon the freedom of the press and of speech.

The Philanthropist passed from the editorship of Birney to that of Gamaliel Bailey, another prominent and brave abolitionist, who conducted the paper in the same city where it had been destroyed by the mob.[39]   This paper was not carried on without difficulty, however; twice the press was demolished in the hands of Bailey.

Birney always thought those who lived in the city of Cincinnati were in favor of the freedom of the press and had no part in the destruction of his press. He thought the nearness of Cincinnati to Kentucky made it easy for those from that state to come over and lead the contest against him.   The fact that the paper could still be published in the city and that Birney could return without a hand being laid upon him gives color to his contention. Birney did not see, as others who were not so prominent in the slavery crusade saw, that the abolition paper published there, jeopardized the Cincinnati Charleston Railroad and that the economic interests of the city were tied up in this action.

The Philanthropist, like all the other anti-slavery papers, was sent through the mail to actual subscribers.   This paper then is connected with the controversy over the mail.   The *Alabama Watchman* Extra, August 22, 1835, gave an account of a vigilance committee which had been appointed to put a stop to gamblers and blacklegs and to use force to detect any person caught distributing or attempting to distribute the paper known as *The Philanthropist* printed by James G. Birney.[40]   A subscriber in Kentucky, described by the editor as a peaceful and law-abiding man, complained because his paper was not coming to him regularly.   He said that he had been able to get the first number, but now the postmaster would not give it to him.   He suggested that it be sent to another town once a month.[41]   A clergyman in Bracken County, Kentucky, who was a subscriber, asked that his paper not be sent in the future because he could not obtain it from the post office.   He had been able to secure the first few copies but was not

[38] *Xenia, Ohio, Free Press*, August 13, 1836.

[39] Oliver Johnson, *William Lloyd Garrison and His Times*, 32.

[40] *The Philanthropist*, January 1, 1836, quoted from the *Alabama Watchman extra*, August 22, 1835, printed at Athens, Alabama.

[41] *Ibid.*, January 28, 1836.   The name of the subscriber was not given, for the obvious reason that it would have been embarrassing to him.

a public meeting which was held on November 3, 1837, he said that he was impelled to the course which he had taken by a fear of God. He realized the sacrifice which he was making when he pledged himself to continue the contest to the last.[71] He further pledged himself to remain in Alton and die and be buried there if need be.[72] Lovejoy wrote letters to the following towns in reference to reëstablishing the *Alton Observer:* Quincy, Jacksonville, Springfield, Alton, and Chatham. The editor rested his rights upon the laws of the state and nation, and could not and would not yield to any mob. The letters closed with the expression that through the fear of God the supporters of the *Observer* have determined to sustain the laws and guard the freedom of the press.[73]

The friends of free speech in the state of Ohio gave Lovejoy a third press.[74] At almost the same time a meeting was called for the purpose of establishing an anti-slavery society in Alton. These two affairs were not conducive to the peace and harmony of the little Illinois city. The meeting, however, was captured by the pro-slavery forces. In the midst of this turmoil the announcement was made that the new press was about to arrive. This caused even more excitement. Lovejoy and his abolition friend, Bucher, stayed at the warehouse to supervise the storing of the press. The editor and his friend were determined to protect their property.[75] The action of Lovejoy and his associates made it easy for those opposed to the abolition society to attack them. Mayor Krum admitted that a request for protection of their property was made to the common council but the demand was refused.[76] It seemed rather strange that, since a request for aid had been made and since the council itself knew that there was excitement and confusion in the city, it did nothing. The mayor did not say why the request for help was refused; if he had seen fit to do so, the explanation would have been quite interesting. The mayor claimed that he and the police authorities did visit the building after they heard the violence going on there. He placed the blame upon those within the building, for they fired the first

[71] G. Johnson, *op. cit.*, 224.
[72] G. Johnson, *op. cit.*, 225.
[73] Letter from E. P. Lovejoy to E. Young, *Journal of Illinois State Historical Society*, XX, 333.
[74] C. P. Koford, *op. cit.*
[75] *Niles Register*, LIII, 197, quoting the *Alton Spectator*, November 9, 1837.
[76] *Niles Register*, LIII, 197. Mayor Krum gives an interesting account of the riot.

shot and killed the first person. This is probably true, but this affair, it must be understood, might have been avoided if the city common council had been willing to take a little caution.

The fact was that the civil authorities did little to protect the property of the abolitionist or disperse those on either side. This negligence resulted in the death of Elijah P. Lovejoy and Bishop, a member of the group opposed to the Lovejoy interest. This could be looked upon in no other sense than that Lovejoy had given his life for the freedom of the press and the right of every citizen freely to deliver printed matter to those who wished to purchase it.[77]

In general, the papers of the northern states condemned the action of Alton and some of the southern papers were just as outspoken. The *Louisville Herald* stated that spilling of the blood of Lovejoy was far worse than "sowing dragons' teeth" and that every drop would cause a new abolition society to spring up.[78] This paper was as ready as any journal to condemn the abolition publication, but this murder seemed like going a bit too far. It was feared, the paper said, that it could find no justification anywhere in the moral or legal code of either the states or the nation. Many of the pro-slavery papers condemned this attack upon the freedom of the press.[79]

The Columbus, Ohio, *Journal and Register*, speaking editorially, said that it could find no words to paint the abhorrence which it felt at such an outrage on property and person.[80] The editor of this journal was willing to see what the city of Alton would do to redeem its fair name.

There were other condemnations from individuals on the seriousness of the crime. One person, who was prominent at a later date, said Lovejoy was deliberately and systematically hastened to his death for no other reason than that he insisted that slavery was a sin.[81] Lovejoy, he thought, had come to the conclusion that slavery and freedom could not exist in the same place and therefore felt it his duty to destroy slavery.

John Quincy Adams thought such religious men as Lovejoy were often doomed to die as martyrs. Such then was the fate of

---

[77] *Ibid.*, 196.
[78] *Cincinnati Daily Gazette*, November 17, 1836.
[79] N. D. Harris, *op. cit.*, 96.
[80] Columbus, Ohio, *Journal and Register*, November 18, 1837.
[81] Horace Greeley, *Recollections*, 287.

Lovejoy, who had given his life in the cause of human freedom.[82]

The Columbus *Journal* wanted to know what would be done by Alton to punish those who committed this crime. Nothing was accomplished because the court declared it did not have jurisdiction over the matter.[83] The trial amounted to practically nothing, and no one was convicted.

The motive that actuated Lovejoy was religious duty; he felt that it was a call of God to edit his paper and distribute it. Those who were opposed to him knew that to permit the paper to be printed was to allow distribution, which must be prohibited at all hazards. Alton was much too close to St. Louis for a paper of the same type to be started as the one prohibited in the city previously. It was bad judgment which brought on this catastrophe. Had the paper been started in some city farther away from St. Louis it might have fared better. It was especially bad policy which caused Lovejoy and his friend to undertake to defend their press. If they had followed the method of Birney, there would probably have been no loss of life. It must not be overlooked that this was nevertheless a contest over the freedom of the press and the right to use the Federal mail.

[82] Nevins, *Diary of John Quincy Adams*, 489.
[83] *Niles Register*, LIV, 6.

CHAPTER VIII

FROM 1840 TO 1860

In 1840 came the attempt on the part of some members of the anti-slavery society to try to make the work of the society political. The Massachusetts Anti-Slavery Society voted in 1840 to take no part in politics as a party, but to apply the standard of abolition to every candidate regardless of party and to support those who agreed to their principles.[1] The anti-slavery societies were sure that the parties were so evenly divided that they held the balance between them. This Massachusetts society came out in its tenth annual report and condemned Birney for his action of injecting politics into the anti-slavery movement. It insisted that no true abolitionist could vote for Birney. The society went so far as to say that no abolitionist was bound to vote for him. Any abolitionist might support someone else if he felt like doing so.[2] Birney was at the beginning a firm believer in the power of the press but later felt that the political influence was necessary for the welfare of abolition. He became a candidate for the presidency in 1840 and made a very poor showing, due, no doubt, to the lack of support by the abolitionists.[3]

The *New York Tribune* said its readers would be astonished to know that the abolitionists had become so bold that in their meeting in 1841, Gerrit Smith presented an address to the American Anti-Slavery Society advising the slaves to revolt against their masters. The address recommended among other things that the slaves seek a favorable opportunity to escape and take all the things they considered essential to their welfare, such as horses, boats, and food.[4] The society itself passed a resolution that it should solemnly and deliberately proclaim to the nations that no power on earth should compel it to take up arms against the slaves if the slaves should use violence in securing their free-

[1] Massachusetts Anti-Slavery Society, *Tenth Annual Report*, 1841, IX, 42.
[2] *Ibid.*, X, 15.
[3] W. Birney, *James G. Birney and His Times*, 333.
[4] January 29, 1841.

dom. This was an extreme position, for most of the abolitionists simply insisted upon the education of the South as a means of emancipating the slaves.

The South was vigilant and kept its committees intact throughout the period. The purpose of the committees was to protect the slaveholder from the incendiary pages that might escape and be distributed and also from the living apostle who might speak a word of advice to his victims. The censorship was not confined exclusively to the abolition papers but was extended to other papers that seemed in any way to discuss the question of slavery.[5] Such a case was reported by the Foreign Anti-Slavery Society from Virginia. It was reported that a postmaster in that state refused to deliver the *Cincinnati Globe*, a free-soil paper. The reason which he gave was that it was contrary to the laws of the state. Henry Wise, of Virginia, was happy to say that his district did not have a single newspaper and if the abolition papers were kept out the people would not be disturbed.[6]

These committees still made themselves responsible for the papers in various parts of the South and were determined that no abolition papers would be published or distributed in that section. Cassius M. Clay, who lived in the city of Lexington, Kentucky, came under the observance of the vigilance committee of that city. In his paper, the *True American*, was printed in August, 1845, an editorial which said that the Constitution was torn and trampled under foot; justice and good faith in a nation were denied; brute force was substituted in place of a high moral tone. It said also that all the great principles were yielded up, and the people were left without God in the world.[7] This editorial incensed the people of that city very much and a meeting was called to appoint a committee to wait upon Clay and ask him to discontinue his paper. On this same day the committee, composed of B. W. Hudley, Thomas H. Waters, and John W. Hunt, wrote Clay informing him that at the meeting of citizens on August 14, a committee had been appointed to wait on him and a resolution passed demanding that his paper cease immediately. The paper, they said, was agitating the community more than Clay realized and it was for his welfare as well as for that of the city

[5] American Foreign Anti-Slavery *Report*, IX, 65.
[6] *Ibid.*, 66. The district which Wise represented is an agricultural section. There are not many papers in that district at the present time.
[7] *Niles Register*, LXVIII, 408.

that they came to him. The committee said they had to report his action the next afternoon at three o'clock, which gave Clay little time to reply.[8]

Clay, even though he was ill at the time and confined to his bed, replied at once. He accused the mob of waiting until he was sick and could not look after his own business before its members interfered with his paper. Clay said that the meeting was unknown to the law and was secret in both its proceedings and purpose; he said further that his paper had nothing to do with the agitation and violence of that city. He told the committee to go back to those who sent it and inform them that he, Clay, knew his own rights.[9] At the same time he wrote an open letter to the people of Kentucky in which he compared to assassins those who interfered with his rights. He thought he would be safe if the people would stand by him; otherwise he would perish;[10] he realized, however, that he could succeed only if the people were with him.

On August 18, there was another meeting of the citizens of Lexington for the purpose of acting on the answer of Clay. At this meeting a letter was read from Clay. He said that he was concerned about the welfare of the people and would do all he could for their peace and happiness. He also thought it was proper for him to answer at the bar of the people and suggested that nothing more be said in his paper about slavery until such time as he could take over the work of editing the paper himself.[11] He reminded the committee that he was at their mercy, and since he could not defend himself they could do what they pleased with him. This was not satisfactory to Thomas F. Marshall, who denounced the *True American* and demanded its suppression. A resolution was passed asking that the paper cease its publication at once. If this was accomplished peacefully no harm would be done to Clay's property. The paper would be put out of the state and shipped, subject to Clay's orders. At this meeting a committee of sixty persons was appointed to carry out the wishes of the meeting. The members of the committee arrived at the building and found the mayor and the city marshall present. The mayor warned the committee that it was violating the law of the city, but it would not be opposed. After the names

[8] Letter from the committee to Clay August 14, 1845. *Ibid.*, LXVII, 408.
[9] Letter from Clay to the committee on August 15, 1845. *Niles Register*, LXVII, 408.
[10] Letter from Clay to the people of Kentucky, *Ibid.*
[11] Letter from Clay to the citizens, August 18, 1845.

of the members had been called, they were allowed to enter the building. They boxed up the press and shipped it, at Clay's direction, to Cincinnati.[12] Thus the freedom of the press had been denied in Kentucky and the *True American* had been driven from the state.

There were other attempts to suppress papers accused of taking part in the anti-slavery crusade. An attempt was made to suppress the *Baltimore Visitor* as an incendiary paper. Resolutions were introduced in the Maryland legislature requiring the governors to institute proceedings against Dr. Snodgrass Claggett, a representative from that state.[13] Nothing happened, however, other than an assault on the freedom of the press. The citizens of Georgetown, Kentucky, favored the suspension of the *Christian Intelligencer,* a Methodist paper, accused of taking part in the anti-slavery crusade. The editor of the paper denied the accusation and showed that he had spoken against the abolitionists; but this, however, was of no avail and he was forced to close his paper.[14] At Newport, Kentucky, a mob of about thirty entered the printing office of W. S. Bailey, publisher of the *Free South,* and proceeded to wreck his shop. After it had carried out two of the forms in the streets, the girls put out the lights and the mob took out no more of the press and left the place. They, however, warned Bailey that if he did not cease publishing the paper they would destroy the whole office and press.[15] The effort to silence newspapers by violence continued throughout the excited area. The southern and border states were just as determined as they had been in the early period that the papers should not be circulated.

The papers were, no doubt, doing much good from the point of view of the abolitionist. The Massachusetts Anti-Slavery Convention in 1846 could say that there was a willingness to discuss both the facts and philosophy of slavery by the general press of the country. These papers were advocating the same doctrine which the anti-slavery papers had held ten years previous.[16] These same arguments had been denounced by the general press in 1836. In spite of this favorable action on the part of the general press the abolitionists continued to distribute their journals. The *Rich-*

[12] *Niles Register,* LXVIII, 408.
[13] Massachusetts Anti-Slavery Society, *Annual Report,* XV, 27.
[14] *Niles Register,* LXVIII, 408.
[15] *Ibid.,* 408.
[16] Massachusetts Anti-Slavery Society, *Annual Report,* XIV, 57.

mond Virginia Whig said that it had a copy of the *Anti-Slavery Standard* which had been sent to the office of that paper. The *Whig* informs us that it was receiving the *Freeman* and that was about all it could swallow at one meal. This particular number of the *Anti-Slavery Standard* insisted that it would do all it could to help the slaves escape. The *Whig* said that abolitionists might help as much as they pleased; if they were caught within the state of Virginia they would suffer the fate of those who had already been caught.[17] The American and Foreign Anti-Slavery Society reported in 1849 that Dr. Bailey continued to edit his paper, *The National Era,* with an increased success. The weekly circulation was about 12,000 copies and had an exchange with seventy papers.[18] The papers continued to increase and to be sent to the South.

The *Whig* thought that the South was in danger because there was a coalition of the Democrats and the Free-Soil party and because the Democrats had joined with them on their platform.[19] The *Whig* could see this only as a danger because of its political nature. The *Whig* saw clearly, however, by 1849, the difficulty of leaving the censorship of incendiary matter to the postmaster. The postmaster in New England may call a thing incendiary which another may call conservative. This same paper said, speaking editorially, the power did not exist in any magistrate, state or Federal, to violate the sanctity of a sealed letter, under any pretense whatsoever. The objectionable papers circulated in spite of all the efforts of the postmasters and of other officers of the state government. The paper insisted that the effort to determine what should go in the mail and what should come out of the mail was the work of stupid politicians for base party purposes.[20] There was no danger, the editor of the *Whig* thought, that the freedom of speech and the censorship of the post office could ever be affected. There had been attacks upon the Post Office from its organization, and it had withstood the attacks. This paper seemed to think if the political element were taken from the controversy it would cease.

This controversy came into the courts in several places during this period. The Grand Jury of Prince William County, Vir-

[17] March 29, 1849.
[18] Massachusetts Anti-Slavery Society, *Annual Report,* X, 49.
[19] *Richmond Whig,* June 14, 1849.
[20] *Ibid.,* August 9, 1849.

ginia, found a true bill against John Underwood for maintaining by speech that an owner had no right of property in his slaves.[21] He was held to bail in the sum of $500 for his appearance at the November court. This case caused much excitement because it was the first case of the kind in the county and also because Underwood was a justice of the peace.[22] The one fact that made the conviction of Underwood doubtful was that his words were not spoken in the presence of slaves. If the words were not so uttered, conviction would seem like a restriction on the freedom of speech and a determination that the rights of southern men to hold slaves should not be discussed.

Another case came into the courts of Virginia in 1849, and was ruled upon by the Supreme Court of that state. The Sunday before Christmas, Jarvis C. Bacon, a free Negro, preached a sermon from the text: "Ye are the light of the world." At the close of the sermon he quoted that part of the scripture which said, "Christ drove the money changers from the temple." In the course of his explanation of this passage he said that if he were to go to his neighbor's crib and steal his corn that would be bad, but it was worse to keep human beings in bondage all their lives and give them nothing save a few stripes. He was indicted in the circuit court of Grayson County and charged with saying the owners had not the right of property in their slaves. When the trial came up he was found guilty and fined $49.62. He appealed the decision of the court.[23] The case came before the Supreme Court or General Court, as it was then called, on appeal from the Grayson County Court. The witnesses testified that they understood him to refer to slaves. There was a controversy over whether he referred to slaves or not. The defense argued that what was said was used in a sermon and was used for illustration. To forbid one to comment on slavery was a violation of the freedom of speech which was not denied by the constitution of Virginia. The decision of the court was rendered by J. Lomax. Bacon was granted a new trial because the evidence was not sufficient in the

[21] *Cincinnati Daily Gazette*, August 15, 1857.
[22] *The Liberator*, August 28, 1857.
[23] *Grattan Report* (Virginia), VII, 602; Bacon was a Negro. He was indicted under the act of 1847-48 which said, "If a free person writes, prints or causes to be written, with intent to advise or incite Negroes in this state to rebel or make insurrection, or inculcate resistance of property of masters in their slaves, or if he shall knowingly circulate the same, he shall be confined in the penitentiary not less than one nor more than five years." *Code of Virginia*, 1849, CXCVI, Sec. 23, 746.

opinion of the judge. He held that if a man could be indicted for what he said in a sermon it was a restriction on religion and on the press.[24] This was significant because the case was that of a free Negro.

The *Richmond Whig* spoke of South Carolina as "our inflammatory neighbors." This paper said a bellicose act occurred recently in Spartanburg. When a certain Barret of that city was accused of circulating a publication forbidden by the laws of that state he was arrested.[25] While he was on trial a letter came from one Thompson. It was suspected that it was for Barrett. The vigilance committee summoned the postmaster of Spartanburg, George H. Legg, to appear in court and bring the letter. He refused on the ground that he had no right to give a letter to anyone other than the person to whom it was addressed or his authorized agent. The postmaster was arrested and thrown in prison, and he finally complied on order of counsel.[26] The postmaster of Spartanburg wrote to the Postmaster-General to obtain information and to let his chief know that he was in prison. He was answered first by the second assistant Postmaster-General, Fritz Henry Warren, on July 24, 1839. He informed the Spartanburg postmaster that various efforts had been made in Congress to pass laws to prevent the circulation of incendiary publications, but no such law was ever passed. The Postmaster-General was helpless in the matter and the whole subject had been left to the discretion of postmasters under the authority of the state government.[27] Six days later the Postmaster-General wrote to Legg in reply to the letter which had been sent him on July 11, stating that the postmaster of Spartanburg was in prison because he had refused to give a letter to anyone except the person to whom it was addressed or to his agent. As the matter then stood it would seem to involve a question of law and a possible conflict of jurisdiction proper to be settled by the legal tribunals. It had therefore been referred to the Attorney-General of the United States who would communicate to him the proper course to be taken on the subject.[28] The Postmaster-General did not have the authority to re-

[24] *Grattan Report* (Virginia), VII, 607.
[25] *Richmond Whig*, August 9, 1849.
[26] American Foreign Anti-Slavery *Report*, X, 101. Barret was a Northerner in South Carolina getting statistical information for a gazetteer.
[27] American Foreign Anti-Slavery *Report*, X, 101. Post Office Department, Appointment Office, July 24, 1849.
[28] *Ibid.*, C, 101. Post Office, July 30, 1849.

lieve his agent, and the officers of the United States were at the mercy of the law. The authorities of Spartanburg felt that if the postmaster could suppress letters and documents the authorities could bring him into court in carrying out the laws of the state. They were not sure, however, that the Postmaster-General planned to follow this policy. The state must protect itself if the Federal Government thought it proper to attempt to shield its agents with privileges and immunities incompatible with the state law; one of two things must happen, either these agents must leave the service of the government or suffer the penalties of the state law though life itself be forfeited.[29] The *Richmond Whig* said of this action on the part of the citizens of Spartanburg, "they claim the right to take from the post office any matter which they deem incendiary. South Carolina is putting the South in a bad light."[30] This case gives some idea of how far the South would go to close all avenues of escape for the distribution of the anti-slavery papers.

Another case came before the courts of Louisiana in 1850. Michael Read, of West Felicianna, in the Seventh District of Louisiana, was accused of violating the state law of 1850, which made it a crime for anyone to utter words which might cause insurrection among the slaves. Read was indicted and found guilty and sentenced to the penitentiary at hard labor for five years.[31] He appealed to the Supreme Court of Louisiana on a writ of error. The language which he was accused of using was that Negroes were as free as the whites. His statement was construed to mean the slaves and whites of West Felicianna, in the state of Louisiana. He was further accused of saying that this was a free country and that Negroes had no obligation to call any

[29] American Foreign Anti-Slavery *Report*, X, 103.
[30] *Richmond Whig*, July 20, 1840.
[31] *Annual Report* (Louisiana), VI, 227; State of Louisiana vs. Michael Read. The law which he was accused of violating was as follows: "Be it further enacted, that whosoever shall make use of language in any public discourse from the bar, the bench, the stage, the pulpit or any place whatsoever; or whosoever shall make use of language in private discourses or shall make use of signs or of actions, having a tendency to produce discontent among the free colored population of this state; or to excite insubordination among the slaves therein; or whosoever shall knowingly be instrumental in bringing into this state any paper, pamphlet, or book having such a tendency as aforesaid, shall, on conviction thereof before any court of competent jurisdiction, suffer imprisonment at hard labor not less than three years, nor more than twenty-one years, or death at the discretion of the court." This act was approved March 16, 1830. *Laws of Louisiana*, 1830-1831, 70.

man master. This statement was not claimed to be the exact words of Read, but was the sense of what he said. Judge C. J. Eustis thought this was not sufficient. He felt that when a man was put in jeopardy for his life for words spoken, the exact words ought to be given. It was not even claimed that any slaves or persons of color were present, and still further the words were uttered in a public discourse. The judgment in the case was arrested and Read was freed.[32] The courts had been called on to stop the flow of abolition literature in several instances; whenever the cases reached the higher courts of the states they were denied, for it seemed too much like a prohibition upon the freedom of speech.

The year 1856 marked another scare about another supposed Negro uprising. The *New Orleans Picayune* of January 2, 1857, was able to say that the holidays had come and gone and no general uprising had occurred and everyone knows now what many knew then, that there was absolutely no chance for a general uprising and that it could scarcely rise above a local section.[33] There might be some danger, the editor of this paper thought, in sections where intercommunication existed, that incendiary traveling salesmen might teach the worst of these Negroes bad habits. The various fanatical papers in the northern states might reach them; in spite of this there was little danger from an uprising by the Negroes, for the paper said the Negroes were generally contented and would help to put down an insurrection. The *Mississippi Clarion* held the South as much responsible as the North for incendiary material which might cause insurrection because the papers there printed everything about abolition seen in the northern papers. The editor thought the thing might have been handled differently if the conservatives of both sections had taken the affair in hand.[34] The one thing that controlled the action of the South throughout the period under consideration was the fear of slavery uprisings.

The South met in several conventions in the forties and fifties for the purpose of looking after its commercial welfare. At the convention which was held at Knoxville, in 1857, C. H. Campbell of Virginia favored the idea of exempting from taxes one or more slaves in the hands of each slaveholder. The

[32] *Annual Report* (Louisiana), VI, 228.
[33] *The Liberator*, January 23, 1857.
[34] *Anti-Slavery Standard*, September 25, 1858.

purpose of this novel idea was to interest a larger number of Southern people in the institution which he called man's curse and God's blessing.[35]   Still another problem which came before the convention was that of controlling the things which should be said in the textbooks.   A resolution was passed at the Knoxville convention which said that in order to control the educational system there should be established publishing houses in the various cities of the South.   The resolution made provisions for referring this plan to the states so that they might subscribe to the affair and become shareholders along with corporations.   The publishing house would be located in the state which took out the largest amounts of stock.[36]   Each state or corporation could appoint delegates to a convention for the organization of such a company.   Certain books were considered not fit for use in the South.   The *Daily Creole* of April 18 criticized Grinshaw's *History of the United States* as unfit for textbook use in the South.   This book formerly held the foremost place in the public schools of the South; however, the paper was not able to tell whether it held that place in 1847 or not.   The paper was not very anxious that its readers notice the stealthy introduction of abolition in its pages.   The editor saw no reason for the material which the author had put in, and thought that it was inconsistent to make the economic welfare subordinate to slavery.[37]

Carrol's *History of the United States* deserved much praise, one paper of the South thought.   It was written by a Southern scholar and gentleman and printed in a southern city; it appealed to the South for its patronage and was accurate.[38]   It did not condemn southern practices and should be used by southern schools.

The convention which met in Vicksburg in 1849 was for the purpose of caring for the moral, educational, and industrial development of the South just as the one in Knoxville had been. The *Vicksburg Sun* of April 19 said the convention would be made up of the best people of the South and those, for the most part, above suspicion.   The one thing which grew out of this convention

[35] *National Intelligencer*, August 21, 1857.
[36] *Cincinnati Daily Gazette*, August 21, 1857.   Southern gentlemen had been asked to write textbooks at the first convention held earlier at Savannah. They were asked to do this so the minds of the children would not be contaminated.   *The Liberator*, May 15, 1857.
[37] *The Liberator*, May 15, 1857.
[38] *Charleston Mercury*, May 24, 1859.

that concerns us was the resolution passed by it creating a committee on literature. The duty of this committee was to inquire
into the expediency of establishing one or more reviews. The
object was to deal solely with the higher walks of philosophy,
science, art, and literature, and to give information on things
which would be of importance to the South.[39] There is little
doubt that such a review would have been valuable in acquainting
the South with the type and accuracy of textbooks offered for
sale. This never materialized because it was too near the Civil
War, but it can be seen how determined the people in the South
were that the right books should fall into the hands of their children. Their own position in the matter depended upon instilling
into their children the belief that their fathers and the southern
principles were right.

As time went on the South came to the place where it was
ready to call any book which did not have the southern point of
view incendiary. Such a book made its appearance in 1857. Hin-
ton Rowan Helper came from the class known in the South before
the Civil War as "poor whites." He was born in Davie County,
North Carolina, December 27, 1829. His father died when he was
only about one year old. His mother was able to care for the
children with the aid of four slaves. He was able to secure the
type of education which was prevalent in the South for poor
whites and country boys.[40] He went to California in 1841, where
he remained until 1854, when he returned to North Carolina.[41] In
1856 when Helper left the South he had the manuscript of the
Impending Crisis ready but found difficulty in securing a publisher for his book. He tried all the standard publishers, but not
one would take his work. He was only able to get it published
through A. B. Burdick, a book agent rather than a publisher.
Helper had to let the book be issued in Burdick's name and also
insure Burdick against loss.[42] This was the very best offer which
he had and was the only way he could bring his book out.

This book caused considerable excitement in the South and
attracted attention in the North. *The Liberator* called this one of
the most valuable volumes which had been published on the political and financial influence of slavery. For his action Helper had

[39] *Ibid.*, May 17, 1859.
[40] J. S. Bassetts, *Anti-Slavery Leaders in North Carolina*, 12.
[41] *South in the Building of the Nation*, ed. by J. A. Chandler, XI, 472.
[42] J. S. Bassetts, *Anti-Slavery Leaders in North Carolina*, 14.

been exiled from his native state because of fidelity to liberty and truth.[43]   Helper thought he would be mobbed, probably killed, should be return to North Carolina.   This work aroused Senator Hammond of South Carolina to call it a monotonous book, and he proceeded to show the errors in it.   Hammond differed from Helper on the number of slaveholders, for he said the number cited pertained only to families and should be multiplied by five or six.[44] Wolfe, who criticized it, thought the book was too prejudiced to be considered.   He, however, doubted that the South could give birth to one who could so carelessly handle the truth and who was such a rascal.[45]   There was little or no praise for Helper's book coming from the South.   The view of slavery which Helper held was not alone his view.   A citizen of Richmond gives the view that the thing which had held Virginia as well as North Carolina back had been slavery.[46]   It was this criticism of the South by Southerners toward which the South was most hostile.

The *Crisis* was looked upon as political material by the Republican party.   A group of gentlemen in New York City and in other parts of the country were impressed with the idea that the circulation of a large edition of Helper's *Impending Crisis of the South* with valuable statistical information and unanswerable arguments against slavery would not fail to impress the southern non-slaveholders because it was coming from one of their own members.   One hundred thousand copies were to be printed.   The *New York Tribune* could say, by the middle of August, that $4,000 of the $16,000 necessary had already been subscribed and one thousand copies had already been printed.   This project was a political one, and these books were to be distributed in those states where the contest of 1860 was to be fought.[47]   The new Republican party which was coming into favor made use of Helper's book.

The *Norfolk, Virginia, Herald* said, when there was a controversy over Helper's book, that everybody in Virginia had a set of laws for the control of her Negroes bond and free.   The law made it an indictable and punishable offence for anyone to express abolition sentiment in the presence of slaves.   The paper was aware that the North would look upon the enforcement of the laws of

[43] December 25, 1857.
[44] Senator J. H. Hammond, *Address to the People of the South*, 16.
[45] S. M. Wolfe, *Helper's Impending Crisis Dissected*, 77.
[46] *New York Daily Tribune*, August 12, 1859.
[47] *Ibid.*, August 12, 1859.

Virginia as destructive to the welfare of the North and contrary to the Constitution. All that was asked, the paper said, was that strangers coming into Virginia would observe implicit obedience to her laws. If those who came did not plan to obey the law it would be better for them to pack up and leave, for they could expect no immunity for their disobedience.[48] This was plain language, and the paper insisted that if anyone in that state expressed himself as opposed to slavery, he must expect to suffer the consequences. The *Richmond Enquirer,* commenting upon the Attorney-General's opinion, said that it was publishing a most excellent report of the Attorney-General of Virginia on the duty of the Postmaster receiving abolition publications.[49] This opinion was based upon the law passed in 1835 which made it a crime for any postmaster not to give notice when such a book forbidden by law should arrive at his office. The justice of the peace should have the book burned in his presence. If the postmaster should violate this law, he was to be fined two hundred dollars. This law was very elaborate indeed and covered every phase of incendiarism.[50] The postmaster in that community had no choice but to obey the law of Virginia regardless of the law of the United States.

The controversy over Helper's book reached the first session of the Thirty-sixth Congress. The Republican party, before printing Helper's book for distribution in the border states, sought endorsements by outstanding Republican Congressmen. This was a natural thing, and sixty-eight of them signed their names as endorsing the book.[51] Among those signing their names was John Sherman of Ohio, the most prominent member of the Republican party in the House and the leading candidate for the speakership.[52] John B. Clark of Missouri introduced a resolution which said that certain members of the House who were mentioned for the speakership had endorsed Helper's book. The resolution further said that anyone who signed it was not fit to be speaker of the House.[53] This threw that body into great confusion and it took the House eight weeks to organize. Many addresses were made pro and con. The *New York Tribune* insisted that the Republican side must not be held responsible for what had happened

[48] *National Anti-Slavery Standard,* December 10, 1850.
[49] November 20, 1850.
[50] *Code of Virginia,* 1849, 746.
[51] *Globe,* 36th Congress, 1st Session, Vol. 29, I, 16.
[52] W. H. Smith, *A Political History of Slavery,* I, 269. Sherman had signed this book at the request of Governor Morgan of New York.
[53] *Globe,* 36th Congress, 1st Session, Part I, XXIX, 3.

in the House, that the Democrats were responsible. If the Republicans had been patient enough to sit quietly in their seats and let Clark go on until the absent members came in, there would have been no trouble in organizing the House, the *Tribune* thought.[54] There was great hostility toward Helper's book because it was considered in the South that he had betrayed that section.

The arguments given pro and con were bitter and sectional. Another thing which made it much more difficult to organize the House was John Brown's raid.[55] Some held this book as responsible for what happened at Harper's Ferry, but as a matter of fact it is almost certain that Brown had not been influenced by the book, for the motive which seemed to have actuated him was religious zeal.

The whole affair was directed against Sherman. For a long time Sherman did not make any attempt to influence the election, and the votes were constantly in his favor. His brother, W. T. Sherman, who was teaching in Louisiana in 1860, was superintendent of the state military school at Alexandria.[56] He wrote his brother John inquiring why he had signed that paper endorsing Helper's book. W. T. Sherman had hoped that his brother would be elected speaker of the House and thought he would have been if he had not endorsed that book. He knew nothing concerning it except what he saw in the papers and hoped his brother would be for theoretical, not practical abolition.[57] W. T. Sherman could only hope that the argument would not be protracted. John Sherman in his reply informed his brother that what he had said in Congress in the course of debate was that he had endorsed the book without knowing what was in it and thought it was a mere pamphlet.[58] This was perfectly possible, but it does not seem probable that a man would sign a document without knowing what it was about; yet that is what Sherman says he did.

On January 30, 1860, two months after Congress had been in session and after thirty-nine ballots had been taken, Sherman withdrew from the race. Sherman insisted all along his one

[54] December 6, 1853. This, of course, was a Republican paper.
[55] *Globe*, 36th Congress, 1st Session, Part I, XXIX, 5.
[56] Henry Coppe, article in *Appleton Encyclopedia of American Biography*.
[57] *Century Magazine*, XIII, 90.
[58] *Ibid.*, Letter of December 24, 1860. He had signed at the request of Governor Morgan of New York. He had been assured that it was unobjectionable. W. H. Smith, *Political History of Slavery*, I, 269.

object had been to keep the organization of the House from under the control of the Administration.[59] It took five other ballots before anyone could be elected speaker of the House.[60] This closed the contest in Congress over the distribution of Helper's *Impending Crisis*.

The Helper book came before a court in the state of North Carolina for a decision in 1860. Daniel Worth was accused of the delivery of a copy of an incendiary publication to an individual; such a delivery was prohibited by the act of the assembly of that state. The book which he was accused of circulating was Helper's *Impending Crisis*. Worth was a native of Guilford County, North Carolina. He had been a justice of the peace, but later after moving to Indiana, he became a preacher in the Methodist Church. He came back to his home and preached in several places with indifferent success.[61] In December, after Harper's Ferry affair, Worth was brought into court and bound over to the spring term of court. He was charged first with the publication and circulation of extracts from Helper's book and second with the selling and delivering of a copy of the book to George W. Bowman and to others.[62] The defense insisted that the book was not a pamphlet and did not come within the law on incendiary literature. Secondly, that the delivery to Bowman was not circulation within the meaning of the statutes of North Carolina. Finally the book was not delivered to free Negroes or slaves and was not read in their presence; therefore, it was not a violation of the laws of that state. The court of Guilford instructed the jury that the sale and delivery of a bound volume was within the prohibition of the statutes and that the sale and delivery of a volume to George W. Bowman, if done with a wicked intent, was publication and circulation within the meaning of the statutes. This instruction gave little chance for Worth to escape, for it was difficult for him to prove that his intent was not evil; and thus the jury gave its verdict for the state. Worth then appealed his case to the Supreme Court of the state of North Carolina. The case came before the court in the spring of 1860. Judge J. Manly delivered the opinion of the court. He said in some cases books might be passed and not circulated, but the circumstances were important. Therefore he felt

[59] *Globe*, 36th Congress, 1st Session, Part I, XXIX, 634.
[60] *Ibid.*, 650.
[61] J. S. Bassett, *Anti-Slavery Leaders in North Carolina*, 25.
[62] *Jones Report* (North Carolina), VII, 488. State vs. Daniel Worth; *Jones Report* (North Carolina), VII, 488.

it fell within the law of pamphlets, and he sustained the verdict of the court below.[63] Worth was placed under $3,000 bond. He left the state and never returned, so that his bondsmen had to lose. Worth did all he could to repay them.[64] The courts had definitely decided that Helper's book was incendiary so far as North Carolina was concerned.

The contest over the distribution of abolition literature through the mail continued until the Civil War. It was a contest, as the North saw it, over the freedom of speech and, as the South saw it, over the protection of property guaranteed by the Constitution.

[63] *Jones Report* (North Carolina), VII, 488.   State vs. Daniel Worth; *Jones Report* (North Carolina), LII, 493.
[64] J. S. Bassett, *Anti-Slavery Leaders in North Carolina*, 27.

CONCLUSION

The controversy over abolition literature and other material of like nature had its origin in 1835. The papers appeared as early as 1816. It is reasonable to suppose that the flare-up came in 1835 and 1836 and not in 1820, because in the early period the abolition question had attracted no attention; the country was absorbed with other issues such as internal improvement. The uprisings such as the Vesey and Nat Turner Insurrections brought fear to the whole South. The Nat Turner Insurrection came just a little while after the publication of the *Appeal*, edited by David Walker, a free Negro, a journal which definitely urged the Negro to revolt. This pamphlet gave character and tone to the whole anti-slavery movement and was blamed definitely for the Nat Turner insurrection by some of the governors in their official messages. In the midst of this confusion *The Liberator* made its appearance and announced its program.

About the same time abolition societies proclaimed a new program. This program had for its purpose the educating of the people to the wisdom of abolition. The method to be used was the distribution of the anti-slavery papers in the South. This new program ushered in a controversy which lasted until the Civil War. These papers literally flooded the South, and in 1835 a million of them were scattered throughout that section. It is not strange that the South objected to these papers because of their nature.

It is a mistake to regard this controversy as of little or no consequence. The South looked upon it as a species of inter-meddling on the part of the northern citizens. The North looked upon the action of the South as a restriction of its rights, particularly freedom of speech and freedom of the press.

The controversy is tied up with the political and economic welfare of the South. Calhoun brought in his bill to regulate the use of the mail because he, as the leader of the South, must either present a bill or the law which Jackson wanted would pass. He conceived the idea of binding his beloved South on the slavery issue. He also had hopes of binding the South and the West on an economic issue against the prosperous North, but this failed and thus the slavery issue became prominent.

From this controversy developed the policy of the Post Office toward objectionable material. In 1835, the postmasters were allowed to send or keep the papers as they thought best because there was no law to force them to do otherwise. When the contest over abolition material in Congress closed all material not prohibited by law must be sent to its destination. This was the legal side of the question. It was not carried out as the law provided, for individuals still did as they thought best, but a policy was developed for the Post Office Department.

The contest is one of the most important in the whole slavery crusade. It definitely developed sentiment in the North and in the South. The South developed an interest in the protection of its property and a willingness to protect it at all hazards. The North developed an interest in the protection of freedom of speech and of the press.

The contest brought out in bold relief the issue over States' rights and National rights. This is one of the most important controversies which faced Congress before the Civil War. The dispute over the mail lasted three decades. It deserves much more consideration than it has received. It has, to a large extent, been overshadowed by other phases of the antislavery crusade, and this has been considered a very small issue, but this particular issue connects itself with the whole of American history between 1829 and 1860. The question is to be found in the legislative bodies of almost all of the states, in the Congress of the United States, in the President's message, and finally in the courts.

BIBLIOGRAPHY

MANUSCRIPTS AND DOCUMENTS

MANUSCRIPTS IN LIBRARY OF CONGRESS

Chase, S. P., Letters and Papers, 1831-1845.
Green, Duff, Letters and Papers, 1831-53.
Hammond, J. H., Papers and Diary from 1837 to 1865.
McLean, John, Letters and Papers, 1836-1846.
Van Buren, Martin, Letters and Papers from 1829 to 1845.
Jackson Papers, 1826 to 1836.

PRINTED SOURCES

American History Leaflets. 12 volumes. New York, 1892. (Edited by Harvard
    Historical Department.)
American Historical Society Report. Vol. II, 1899; Vol. II, 1918.
Abridgment of Congressional Debates. 12 volumes. New York, 1859 (edited
    by T. H. Benton).
Congressional Globe, 1836 to 1860. Washington, D. C.
Congressional Globe Appendix, 1836 to 1860. Washington, D. C.
House Journal, 1835 to 1840. Washington, D. C.
Messages and Papers of the Presidents. 10 volumes (edited by Richardson;
    Washington, 1896).
Register of Debates, 1832 to 1837. Washington (edited by Gales and Seaton).
State Documents on Federal Relations. 5 volumes. Philadelphia, 1906.
Senate Journal, 1835 to 1837. Washington, D. C.
Statutes at Large. Volume V. Boston, 1846.

STATE LAW AND COURT REPORTS

Acts of the General Assembly of the Commonwealth of Virginia. Richmond,
    1832.
Acts of the General Assembly of Georgia, 1835 and 1836. Milledgeville, 1835.
Acts of the General Assembly of North Carolina, 1833-34 and 1835-36. Ra-
    leigh, 1836.
Acts of a Public Nature of State of Tennessee. Nashville, 1832.
Acts and Resolutions of the Assembly of South Carolina, 1833. Columbia,
    1833.
Digest of Laws of State of Alabama. Tuscaloosa, 1843. (Edited by C. Clay.)
Digest of Law of Alabama. Philadelphia, 1833. (Edited by John G. Aekien.)
Journal of House of Representatives of State of Ohio. Columbus, 1835.
Laws of Kentucky, 1835. Frankfort, 1836. (Edited by J. T. Morehead.)
Laws of Maryland. Annapolis, 1836.
Laws of Mississippi, 1836. Jackson, 1836.
Laws of Missouri, 1836-37. Jefferson City, 1837.
Laws of State of New York. Albany, 1836.
Laws of Tennessee, 1836. Nashville, 1836.
Official Manual of State of Missouri, 1889-1890. Jefferson City, 1899.
*Report of Cases Argued and Determined in Court of Appeals and General
    Court of Virginia.* Richmond, 1840. (Edited by B. W. Leigh.)
Report of Cases Decided by Court in Bank, 1837-1838. Columbus, Ohio, 1838.
    (Edited by C. Hammond.) Ohio i.

Hume, J. F., *Abolitionist* together with personal memoirs of the struggle for Freedom. New York, 1905.

Legare, H. S., *Legare's Writings in 2 volumes*. Charleston, South Carolina, 1845 (edited by his son).

Lovejoy, Joseph and Owen, *Memoirs of Rev. Elijah P. Lovejoy*. New York, 1838. (Introduction by J. Q. Adams.)

Mansfield, E. D., *Personal Memoirs Social, Political and Literary*. 1802-1843. Cincinnati, 1879.

Marsh, Luther R., *Writings and Speeches of Alvan Stewart on Slavery*. New York, 1860.

Martineau, Harriet, *Views of Slavery and Emancipation from Society in America*. New York, 1837 (printed separately).

May, Samuel J., *Memoirs of Samuel Joseph May*. Boston, 1873. (Edited by Thomas J. Mumford.)

May, Samuel J., *Recollections of Our Anti-Slavery Conflict*. Boston, 1869.

Mayo, Robert, M.D., *Political Sketch of Eight Years in Washington in Four Parts*. Baltimore, 1837.

Mercury's Course and the Right of Discussion. Charleston, 1857. (Compiled by I. W. Haynes.)

Moore, J. B., *The Works of James Buchanan* (Comprising his speeches, State Papers, and Private Correspondence). 12 volumes. Philadelphia, 1908.

Olmstead, Frederick L., *A Journey in Seaboard Slave States*. New York, 1856.

Pierce, E. L., *Memoirs and Letters of Charles Sumner*. 3 volumes, 1835-1860.

Prentiss, S., *Memoir*. New York, 1886.

Rankin, John, *Letters on American Slavery Address to Thomas Rankin*. Boston, 1838.

Sargent, Nathan, *Public Men and Events*. 2 volumes. Philadelphia, 1876.

Taney, R. B., *Memoirs*. Baltimore, Maryland, 1872 (edited by Samuel Taylor).

Thomas, A. A., *Correspondence of Thomas Ebenezer Thomas*. Dayton, Ohio, 1909. (Deals with anti-slavery struggle in Ohio.)

Tyler, L. G., *The Letters and Times of the Tylers*. Richmond, Virginia, 1884.

Willen, G. W. F., *An Argument on the Unconstitutionality of Slavery*. Boston, 1841.

Webster, Daniel, *The Writings and Speeches of Daniel Webster*. 18 volumes (National Edition), Boston, 1903.

BIOGRAPHIES AND AUTOBIOGRAPHIES

Austin, George L., *The Life and Times of Wendell Phillips*. Boston, 1901.

Bancroft, Frederick, *The Life of William H. Steward*. New York, 1900. 2 volumes.

Birney, William, *James G. Birney and His Times*. New York, 1890.

Blaine, James G., *Twenty Years of Congress*. From Lincoln to Garfield. 2 volumes. Norwich, Connecticut, 1884. (Gives the events which lead up to the war.)

Claiborne, J. F. H., *Life and Correspondence of John A. Quitman*. 2 volumes. New York, 1860.

Claiborne, J. F. H., *Seventy-five Years in Old Virginia*. Washington, New York, 1904.

Clarke, J. F., *Anti-Slavery Days*. New York, 1884.

Coleman, Chapman, Ann Mary Butler (Grittenden). 2 volumes. Philadelphia, 1875.

Curtis, George T., *Life of James Buchanan*. 2 volumes. New York, 1883.

Curtis, G. T., *Life of Daniel Webster*. 2 volumes. New York, 1893.

Davis, V. H., *Jefferson Davis, Ex-President of the Confederate States of America*.

Garland, Hugh A., *Life of John Randolph of Roanoke.* 2 volumes. New York, 1850.

Gilmer, G. H., *Sketches of Some of the First Settlers of Upper Georgia.* New York, 1855.

Frothingham, O. S., *Garret Smith, a Biography.* New York, 1879.

Greeley, H., *Recollections of a Busy Life.* New York, 1868.

Hart, A. B., *Salmon Portland Chase.* (American Statesmen), Boston, 1899.

Hunt, G., *John C. Calhoun* (American Crisis Series). Philadelphia, 1908.

Jenkins, *Life of John C. Calhoun.* Auburn, 1850.

Jervey, T. D., *Robert Y. Hayne and His Times.* New York, 1909.

Johnson, Oliver, *William Lloyd Garrison and His Times.* Boston, 1882.

Julian, G. W., *The Life of Joshua R. Giddings.* Chicago, 1892.

Lodge, H. C., *Daniel Webster* (American Statesmen). New York, 1898.

Lundy, Benjamin, *The Life Travels and Opinions of Benjamin Lundy.* Philadelphia, 1847.

Miegs, William, *Life of John C. Calhoun.* Boston, 1917.

Morse, John T., Jr., *John Q. Adams* (American Statesmen). Boston, New York, 1898.

Morris, B. F., *The Life of Thomas Morris* (pioneer and long a legislator of Ohio and Senator). Cincinnati, 1856.

Parish, John C., *Robert Lucas* (Iowa Biographical Series edited by B. B. Shambaugh). Iowa City, Iowa, 1906.

Roosevelt, Theodore, *Life of Thomas Hart Benton* (American Statesmen). Boston, New York, 1887.

Schurz, Carl, *Life of Henry Clay.* 2 volumes. (American Statesmen). Boston, New York, 1887.

Seward, W. H., *Life and Public Service of John Q. Adams.* Auburn, 1849.

Seward, W. H., *Autobiography.* 6 volumes. (The Memoirs of his life are given from 1831-1846; of value to the study of slavery.) New York, 1877.

Shield, Joseph D., *Life and Times of Sergeant Smith Prentiss.* Philadelphia, 1884.

Shipp, J. E. D., *Giant Days or Life and Times of William H. Crawford.* Embracing excerpt from his Diary, Letters and Speeches. Amercus, Georgia, 1909.

Story, William, *Life and Letters of Joseph Story.* 2 volumes. Boston, 1851.

Sumner, W. G., *Andrew Jackson as a Public Man* (American Statesmen). Boston, 1885.

Tappan, Lewis, *The Life of Arthur Tappan.* New York, 1870.

Van Holst, E., *John C. Calhoun* (American Statesmen). Boston, 1882.

Warden, R. B., *An Account of the Private Life and Public Service of Salmon Portland Chase.* Cincinnati, Ohio, 1874.

Weed, Thurlow, *Autobiography.* 2 volumes (edited by Harriet A. Weed). Boston, 1883.

Wise, Barton H., *The Life of Henry A. Wise of Virginia, 1860 to 1876.* New York, 1899.

Wright, Elizur, *Myron Holly and What He Did for Liberty.* Boston, 1882.

Articles in Periodicals

American Historical Review, VI, 1901, and XXXIV, Number 2, 1929. The Economic Background of the Liberty Party, J. P. Bretz.

Appeal (edited by David Walker), Boston, Massachusetts. 1830 Revised Edition.

Century Magazine, Vol. 23, November, 1892-93.

The Examiner and Journal of Political Economy. Philadelphia, 1835. Several articles on States' Rights.

Illinois State Historical Society Journal, 10-27, II, 4 Letters of Elijah P. Lovejoy, 1837.

Randall, C. E., and Tyan, Daniel, *History of Ohio: The Rise and Progress of an American State*. New York, 1912.

Rhodes, J. F., *History of the United States from the Compromise of 1850*. 8 vols. New York, 1902.

Schuler, James, *History of the United States under the Constitution*. 6 vols. Washington, D. C., 1889.

Simms, H. H., *The Rise of the Whigs in Virginia, 1824-1840*. Richmond, Va., 1929.

Smith, W. H., *A Political History of Slavery*. 2 vols. New York, 1903.

Stanwood, E. A., *History of the Presidency from 1786-1915*. 2 vols. New York and Boston, 1928. (There have been several reprints since it first came out in 1896.)

Steiner, B. C., *History of Slavery in Connecticut*. Baltimore, 1893 (Johns Hopkins University Historical and Political Science Series).

Stroud, George M., *Sketch of Laws Relating to Slavery in the Several States of the United States of America*. Philadelphia, 1827.

Swany, C. B., *Episcopal Methodism with Sidelights on Ecclesiastical Politics*. Boston, 1926.

Taylor, H., *The Origin and Growth of the American Constitution*. Boston and New York, 1911.

Thomas, W., *The Enemies of the Constitution Discovered*. New York, 1835.

Treadwell, S. B., *American Liberties and American Slavery, Morally and Politically*. New York and Boston, 1838.

Tremain, Mary, *Slavery in the District of Columbia*. (The Policy of Congress and Struggle for Abolition.) New York and London, 1892.

Trent, W. P., *Southern Statesmen of the Old Regime*. Boston and New York, 1897.

Turner, E. R., *The Negro in Pennsylvania*. Baltimore, 1910.

Van Holst, Dr. H., *The Constitutional and Political History of the United States*. 8 vols. Chicago, 1888.

Watkins, J. L., *King Cotton: An Historical and Statistical Review, 1790-1908*. New York, 1908.

Whitfield, T. M., *Slavery Agitation in Virginia, 1829-1832*. Baltimore, 1930.

Williams, George W., *History of the Negro Race in America, 1619-1880*. 2 vols. New York, 1883.

Williams, W., and Shoemaker, F. L., *Missouri, Mother of the West*. 5 vols. Chicago and New York, 1930.

Wilson, H., *History of Rise and Fall of Slave Power in America*. Boston and New York, 1872. 3 vols.

Wise, Henry A., *Seven Decades of the Union*. Philadelphia, 1872.

Wolfe, S. M., *Helper's Impending Crisis Dissected*. Philadelphia, 1860.

Anonymous, *The Soldier, The Battle and Victory*. Cincinnati, 1852. (Fanaticism and Its Results or Facts versus Fancies.) Baltimore, 1860.

MASTERS' THESES AT OHIO STATE UNIVERSITY

McKee, J. W., *The Attitude of John Q. Adams toward Slavery*, 1931.

Meredith, W. J. F., *The Negro in the Anti-Slavery Movement*. 1930.

INDEX

INDEX

A

Alabama, law of 1832, 57, 58
"Alabama Watchman," extra, August 22, 1833, 99
Abolition, of slavery in District of Columbia, 102, 104; societies, 91, 95
Abolitionist, 49; Ohio, 49, 50; New York Legislature, 50, 51; New York Resolutions, 52
Act of 1812, 102
Adams, John Q., 104, 107
"Alton Observer," 106
American Anti-Slavery Society, reports, 9; program, 9, 10, 19, 62
Anti-Abolitionist Party, 41; warning of, 95; meeting of July 23rd, 95
Anti-Slavery Magazines, 92; meeting in Cincinnati in 1836, 94; records, 10, 13, 15, 92; society, 106
"Argus," 89
Armstrong, Samuel, Lieutenant-Governor address of 1836, 52

B

Bacon, Jarves C., a free Negro indicted for saying men had not the right of property in slaves, 114
Bailey, Gamalied, takes over the *Philanthropist*, 99
Bailey, W. S., publisher of *Free South*, 112
Baptist, Richard, letter to Van Buren, 86
Barbour, James, letter to Henry Clay, 90
Barrett case, 1839, 102
Benton, Thomas H., against bill on incendiary publications, 76, 78, 80, 81
Birney, James G., organization of auxiliary to American Anti-Slavery Society, 92; established the *Philanthropist*, 93; publishing of paper, 94; appeal to Mayor, 95; response to committee, 96; destruction of press, 97; method compared with Lovejoy, 108
Blakely, M., letter to Van Buren, 87
Blanding, Abraham, connection with railroad, 69
Bowman, George W., 123
Breckenridge, Rev. R. J., 100
Brown, John, raid, 122
Buchanan, James, on circulation of incendiary papers, 75, 76, 77

Burdick, A. B., publisher of Helper's *Impending Crisis*, 119
Burt, Amistead, a Calhoun democrat, 74
Butler, B. F., Attorney-General of United States, 88

C

Calhoun, John C., report on incendiary papers in Senate, 63, 64, as a Nationalist during War of 1812, 65; suggesting need for special committee, 66, 67; as a member of special committee, 68; projecting the Charleston-Cincinnati railroad, 69; on slavery, 70; congressional laws in relation to state laws, 71, 72, 73, 74; on "States' Rights," 75; opposition to administration, 76, 77, 82; on bill concerning incendiary publications, 78, 80; on the political issue, 83
Calhoun, Mrs. Anna C., 74
Carter, citizen of Georgia, 69
Charleston post-office attacked, controversy, 15-25
Chase, Salmon P., 98
Cincinnati papers, *Republic*, 93-94; *Whig*, 97
Citizen's Committee, resolution published by, 97, 98
Clark, John B., resolution, 121, 122
Clay, Cassius, editor of *True American*, 109; reply to mob, 111
Clay, Henry, reference to reports, 71; against bill on incendiary publications, 76, 77, 78; supporting an amendment, 79; political campaign, 83
Clayton, Senator of Delaware, 67
Clinton, Governor of New York, annual message, 89
Coffin, Levi, opinion of mob against Birney, 94
Collier, Judge, decision in McDonald case, 102
Columbus, Georgia, Enquirer, 89
Committee of twenty-one, 1835, and abolitionist papers, in Charleston, 28
Common Council, Alton, 106
Compromise of 1850, 88
Congress, 24th, 61, 73
Controlling the Abolition papers, views of the *Richmond Whig*, 43; threat of *Southern Patriot*, 43; as

β